The Best of AskTheCollegeGuy.com

Parental Guidance <u>NOT</u> suggested

by

"The College Guy"

authorHOUSE™

1663 Liberty Drive, Suite 200
Bloomington, Indiana 47403
(800) 839-8640
www.AuthorHouse.com

First published by AuthorHouse 03/11/05

ISBN: 1-4208-4023-1 (sc)

Printed in the United States of America
Bloomington, Indiana

This book is printed on acid-free paper.

INTRODUCTORY WARNING:
This book is NOT like other college books.

Most college books out there are written by professors, psychologists, sociologists, or college administrators. But, rather than writing for college students and/or soon-to-be college students, these other books seem to be written for parents! Since history has shown that most college-related books are actually purchased by parents (as gifts for their college-aged kids), it makes good financial sense for authors to adjust their writing styles to target parents in an effort to sell more books. But, to be perfectly honest, **we think that sucks!**

If you're a college student, a soon-to-be college student, or a recent college graduate, then we guarantee this will be the best college-related book you've ever read. Unfortunately, we also predict that most of your parents will hate it because we will likely shatter their naive view of what college is really like these days – and we might use an occasional "bad word" or two in the process.

We address *real* topics and answer *real* questions, from *real* college students across the country. We talk about college life the way it *really* is, **without sugar-coating it for Mommy and Daddy.**

We recognize that this approach might hurt our book sale totals if parents are shocked or offended by anything we write and are therefore reluctant to buy our book for their kids. But, whatever, we refuse to sell out and change our writing to appease naive or oversensitive parents.

We'd prefer to roll the dice and count on friend-to-friend recommendations to spread the word about our book, and maybe hope that older siblings or cool aunts and uncles will see our book as the perfect graduation gift.

INTRODUCTORY DISCLAIMERS:

This book is not intended for parents, professors, campus administrators, or anyone who clings to the asinine notion that college students spend all their time going to class, studying, and innocently playing board games in their room.

Our lawyer warned us against discussing such topics as underage drinking or pre-marital sex; we promptly fired that lawyer. We write about college life the way it REALLY is - not the way parents, professors, and campus administrators would like it to be. Denying the existence of things like under-age drinking and pre-marital sex on college campuses is like denying Anna Nicole Smith's breast implants, Michael Jackson's nose job(s), and Barry Bonds' steroid use. Kid yourself if you want, but we prefer reality.

The AskTheCollegeGuy.com website, and this corresponding book, provide humor and *semi*-serious advice -- **for entertainment purposes only!** If you are in dire need of completely serious answers or advice, please consult a trained professional. When it comes to serious advice, AskTheCollegeGuy.com is about as professional as Miss Cleo or a Magic 8-Ball.

We accept no liability for anything resulting from our so-called "advice," particularly if you don't understand sarcasm and you suffer a serious injury after we tell you to "run full-speed into a brick wall" or "attempt to shove your head back up your ass where it belongs." *[Editors' Note: If you do run full-speed into a brick wall or attempt to shove your head up your ass, please feel free to send us pictures of the effort]*

There are two kinds of people in this world: people who tell you what you want to hear and people who tell you what you need to hear. AskTheCollegeGuy.com not only tells you what you need to hear, but we extend the added courtesy of telling you how dumb you are for not knowing it already.

You can always contact us at editors@AskTheCollegeGuy.com. All submitted materials become the property of AskTheCollegeGuy.com and if you send us a question or comment, you agree to be publicly subjected to whatever critical, demeaning, and sarcastically opinionated response we deem appropriate. Anyone who is ever pissed off or offended by anything we write is free to:

a) burn our book (as long as you buy it first)

b) write your own damn book

c) email your complaints to DelusionalOversensitiveReaders@askthecollegeguy.com.

TABLE OF CONTENTS

POP QUIZ:

We know how much everybody hates tests and quizzes, but this is our book and we can do whatever we want, so we're going to start you off with a quick multiple-choice question anyway:

What is the significance of the number 18?

A) The age (18) to which AskTheCollegeGuy.com firmly believes the legal drinking age should be changed?

B) The year (as in "1918") that the Boston Red Sox had last one a World Series prior to AskTheCollegeGuy.com correctly picking them to win it all in 2004?

C) The birthday (18th) that horny guys everywhere are desperately – and inexplicably – waiting for the hottie-teen-celebrity-of-the-month to celebrate?

[Editors' Note: The whole "count the days until they're 18 and legal" thing is really an inexplicable phenomenon. Think about it. There's no age-law on fantasies, so why do guys really care when they actually turn 18? Did you hook up with Mary-Kate and Ashley when they turned 18? Did you get lucky with Lindsay Lohan when she turned 18? And, we're sorry to disappoint you but, you're probably not getting a shot with Britney's little sister Jamie-Lynn Spears when she turns 18 (on April 4, 2009) either!]

D) The percentage (18%) of all questions we receive each August/September (primarily from new freshmen) which relate to homesickness.

E) The number of months (18) that a chicken named Mike survived AFTER having his head chopped off back in the 1940's. 18 months without a head!?!? [Note: Mike's owner fed and watered the headless chicken directly into his gullet using an eyedropper. Tragically, Mike eventually choked to death one night in an Arizona motel room. True story!]

F) All of the above.

Ah, how appropriate, the correct answer is "F".

But, unfortunately, only answer D is relevant to the following question/answer (not that we couldn't devote an entire column to Lindsay Lohan, Mary-Kate and Ashley, and our fantasy of what might transpire if they were all locked in a room together with nothing but 8 bottles of wine, a king-sized bed, romantic mood music, a box of feathers, and a bathtub full of orange Jello).

Anyway, there was absolutely no point to all of that except to take a long-winded approach to explaining that 18% of the questions we receive during the first month of each year are related to homesickness, which leads into our first question of Chapter 1...

Chapter One
-SEPTEMBER-

QUESTION:
My daughter is homesick. Besides telling her it is normal and when classes start she will meet people, what should I do? She is calling me 4 times a day and crying. She has gone to her seminars and she is at least moving around, but still crying. Should I go for a visit and bring her things from home?

-- Momma D,
A caring mom whose daughter is homesick at Rutgers

[Editors' Note: Please be aware that we chose to start the book with this question because it was a question of great historical significance. Throughout our existence, this is the ONLY question AskTheCollegeGuy.com has ever answered from a parent. For starters, there aren't too many parents who even read our column in the first place. And any e-mails we do receive from parents are usually written by naive parents who are certain that their son or daughter has never been drunk, would never skip a class, and would never even consider having premarital sex. So these parents end up hating us when we shatter their pristine image of their perfectly innocent sons and daughters by explaining what really goes on at college. So anyway, we've never had a question from a parent that was really worth acknowledging.... until now!]

ANSWER:

Dear Momma D.,

So your homesick daughter is calling you four times a day? In that case, your duty as a caring, loving mother requires you to do one thing and one thing only... you must change your phone number and make it unlisted so that crying little brat-of-a-daughter can never find you again.

Ok, sorry, we didn't really mean that; it's just hard sometimes to restrain our inner-wiseass from leaping out into an answer. Anyway, if you don't like that suggestion, we've got plenty more advice and wisdom to share with you...

We think that the next best way to address this situation is to heed the wise words of an ancient philosopher who once said:

> *"You only get one shot,*
> *do not miss your chance to blow,*
> *this opportunity comes once in a lifetime.*
> *You'd better lose yourself in the... moment."*

Momma D., you're probably not familiar with the teachings of this particular philosopher, but he was also the all-knowing clairvoyant who proudly proclaimed: "I'm Slim Shady, yes, I'm the real shady. All you other slim shady's are just imitating."

Anyway, the "one shot" and one "opportunity" that Mr. Shady is referring to in the inspirational passage above is the first few weeks of college. That's right, the first few weeks of college collectively constitute a phenomenon like no other, an opportunity to start fresh and make friends in an environment with hundreds, if not thousands, of other freshmen who don't know anybody either. *[For more on this phenomenon, see "The Magical Month," a few pages ahead]*

Momma D., would you waive a cheeseburger in the face of somebody on a diet? No? Then do NOT go visit your homesick daughter and bring her things from home! She needs to be at school, interacting with all the other freshmen, and she needs to be focused on meeting people and making friends. Remind her that she only gets one shot, one opportunity, to seize everything she ever wanted. Will she capture it? Or let it slip? And when she asks where the hell you got that from, tell her it was from your good friend Eminem. She'll either cheer up immediately because she'll think she has the coolest mom in the world, or she'll cheer up because her problems will seem insignificant in comparison to her mom who is apparently going through a mid-life crisis.

Anyway, for Momma D., her daughter, and all the other homesick students out there who don't feel this question sufficiently addressed the issues of homesickness with sufficient advice, we agree. Please take a look at the question a few pages ahead for a more serious response with more practical advice on how to get over homesickness. And Momma D., be sure to pass the advice from the next few pages on to your daughter - and make sure she tells all her friends at Rutgers about AskTheCollegeGuy.com. Oh, wait, we forgot she doesn't HAVE any friends there yet. Sorry, we forgot about that part.

-- *The College Guy*

P.S. For those of you who like the fact that we were somehow able to use Eminem as the basis for answering a question about college homesickness, tune in next week as 50 Cent teaches us how to drink Bacardi like it's our birfday.

QUESTION:

How do you get a lightbulb out of your ass without it breaking?

-- Anal Retentive, SUNY Albany

ANSWER:

Well, that depends on how you got the light bulb *in* your ass without breaking it. (Oh how proud Thomas Edison would be!)

Anyway, we here at AskTheCollegeGuy.com have only limited experience having anything stuck in or up our ass (with the noted exception of the occasional latex-gloved finger of the AskTheCollegeGuy.com in-house physician), so we can only offer our best guess. As you must be in incredible pain, or at least feeling socially awkward, we will skip the obvious "How many jackasses does it take to screw a light bulb up their ass?" jokes and get straight to the point.

We suggest you make your way down to the school cafeteria on Mexican Fiesta night (a.k.a. road-kill night), and gorge yourself like a man possessed by the taste of possum. When you have finished eating, drink a triple shot of espresso, a six pack of Beast Lite, and top it all off with a bottle of prune juice. Not only is this mixture guaranteed to blow the lid off your ass, dislodging any inappropriately misplaced household items in the process, but it is also likely to cause temporary blindness, the removal of any unwanted ass-hair, and the hallucination that you are the reincarnated soul of Scrooge McDuck. We wish you the best of luck with your 60-watt extraction procedure, and please, once the bulb has been removed, feel free to shove your head back up your ass where it belongs.

-- The College Guy

QUESTION:
I'm looking forward to college but everyone keeps telling me how hard the works is. Will I have any time to work or hangout besides studying? Is the work really THAT impossible? What should I expect from college?

-- Rae, Ball State University

ANSWER:
Who's telling you how hard college is? Your parents? Let's keep in mind that they're the same people who told you about Santa Claus and the Tooth Fairy.

Ok, let's play Jeopardy for a minute. The Answer is: "Shit, Shower, and Shave." The question is: "What are the 3 most important "S"-tasks to take care of before a big night out?" *[Note: The shaving part would refer to legs and pits for girls, face for guys, and all of the above for your grandmother.]*

So what do those 3 S's have to do with your question? Well, nothing... except that we're about to give you a new set of "s" words to think about.

Like Mr. Miyagi tells Daniel-sahn in Karate Kid, it's all about balance. You're not painting the fence or sanding the floor, but you *are* going to have to balance your S's.

Studying – You're probably not paying thousands of dollars in tuition just to screw around, party 24-7, and improve upon your personal best of a 30-second keg stand. *[Editors' Note: In most cases, it's your parents who are paying thousands of dollars in tuition for you to screw around, party 24-7, and improve upon your personal best of a 30-second keg stand.]* Anyway, regardless of who's paying, your studies are obviously a big part of why you're in college in the first place. So, to put yourself in the best position to actually make it through to graduation, you've got to appropriately allocate some time for studying (and you've got to drag your hung-over ass out of bed each morning and actually go to your classes).

Socializing -- While your academics are important, no college experience is complete without a significant amount of socializing. You might not want to acknowledge this to your professors or your parents, but we promise you will learn just as much - if not more - from your social experiences outside the classroom than from your academic experiences inside the classroom. Making friends, hanging out, goofing off, getting drunk, hooking up... the social times and the random experiences you will have throughout college are a big part of how you're going to learn about yourself, about different kinds of people, and about life in general. As stated above, your studies are important, but definitely don't bury yourself in books, lock yourself in the library all year, and forget to look around and have some fun once in a while.

Sports -- [For the record: No matter how competitive your drinking games may get, Quarters, Beer-Pong, and Asshole do NOT qualify as sports.] It is extremely important that you stay active at college. You can't all be varsity athletes, but there aren't too many colleges out there that don't have a gym, a track, or athletic fields - and intramural sports are huge on most campuses. So there's really no excuse not to make some time for sports and exercise. Find a workout-buddy to run with or to hit the gym with and make it a part of your regular schedule. The "freshman fifteen" didn't come out of nowhere; beer and late-night pizza delivery is a killer. And just in case you were wondering... even if you run to the front door to get your pizza from the delivery guy, it does NOT count as exercise.

Sleep -- No explanation is needed here. You know what sleep is. You know you need it. Make sure you get enough sleep - but don't overdo it and become that lazy sack of crap who sleeps 18 hours a day.

By this point in your life, you don't think twice about finding time to shit, shower, and shave before going out.... now you just have to find time for studying, socializing, sports, and sleep in college. It's all about balance - Ay, Daniel-sahn.

           -- The College Guy

QUESTION:
Hey College Guy, I think my roommate is going to suck! I spoke with her on the phone this summer and she seems like such a loser! We have nothing in common! There's no way we can be friends. Any advice?

         -- Dreading The Upcoming Year,
              A small school in California

ANSWER:
So you're judging your roommate on a first impression? Well, then how about we judge you on a first impression; we think you're a snobby, judgmental, little bitch! And if you're right about your roommate being a loser, then you're probably mistaken about not having anything in common because you don't sound too cool yourself.

Ok, maybe that was a little harsh. Sorry. Writing an advice column with a hangover isn't as easy as you'd think.

Anyway, thinking that you have to become best friends with your roommate in order to have a good year and/or pre-judging your roommate because they're a little different are two common mistakes made by college students, particularly new freshmen. *And speaking of mistakes made by freshmen, we figured we'd take this opportunity to give you tips regarding two of the most common mistakes made by incoming freshmen. *[Editors' Note: ... and to start off the Double-Jeopardy round, we'll take "Transitional Stretches That Allow Us To Ignore Your Question And Write About What WE Want To" for $400, Alex.]*

"Shower shoes? Why do I need shower shoes?"
Nothing says "Welcome to College" like an itchy, crusty case of athlete's foot! So if you share a community shower, make sure you've got a designated pair of shower shoes (a.k.a. flip-flops), because remember, you're definitely not the only one who's ever pissed [or worse!] in the shower.

"College is gonna be awesome! I'm gonna to hook up with as many people as I can!"
Sounds good in theory, right? Unfortunately, the first few weeks of school are when many less-than-flattering reputations are developed. Don't let yourself become "that sleazy, wanna-be-player guy who tried to hook up with every girl in your dorm " or "that skanky, slutty ho who spends the night at a different fraternity house each night." No matter how big your school might seem, rumors and gossip spread faster than a computer virus on speed. Privacy is virtually non-existent when it comes to who has hooked up with whom. And, ironically, you'll find these reputations are often as hard to get rid of as the STD you likely picked up while building your dirty new rep.

-- The College Guy

QUESTION:
OK, I know it's only been a few days, but I'm really really homesick - any advice?

-- Missing My Mommy,
Clark-Atlanta University

ANSWER:
First of all, take some initial comfort in knowing that you are not alone. There are plenty of other students at your school, in your dorm, even on your hall/floor that are experiencing the exact same homesickness that you are.

So how do you know for sure that you're really not alone and that others are homesick too? Well, because that's what we just told you and we're professionals who know our shit! Besides, you're just a homesick little freshman missing your mommy, so don't argue with us, damn it!

Seriously though, you need to understand that being homesick is pretty frickin' common. The idea of being in a new place where you don't know anyone is obviously going to be scary - not quite as scary as the image of your grandmother giving lap-dances wearing a push-up bra and a thong, but scary nonetheless. *[Pause... pause... get that visual image of your grandma at a strip club... ok, now you can continue reading]*

Anyway, so what are you going to do to get over this homesickness? Oh, right, that's what you're asking us. Well, while there's no harm in calling home once in a while, cuddling with a childhood stuffed animal, or reminiscing over a high school yearbook or prom pictures, this really won't do anything to help you get adjusted to your new life at college (and it won't win you any "cool points" with an unsympathetic new roommate either). So we have three pieces of time-tested advice:

1) Take advantage of the magical month.
2) Keep your damn door open.
3) Get involved.

Ok, fine, we'll elaborate…

1) The Magical Month - The first month of school is a phenomenon like no other. The vast majority of people in your dorm and in your classes (assuming they are also freshmen) will be in the exact same situation as you in the sense that they will have arrived on campus without knowing anyone either. Everybody is looking to meet people and make friends.

In almost any other environment that your life will ever put you in, it is difficult and/or awkward to walk up to a random person and introduce yourself (at least when you're sober). But during your first days/weeks on campus, you NEED to do it. You don't need anything clever (and definitely avoid anything even remotely resembling a pickup line). Just walk up to people and say "Hi, I'm Sarah" or "Hey, what's up? I'm Joey." *[Editors' Note: These specific introductions are only recommended if your name happens to be Sarah or Joey. Otherwise we suggest you slightly alter the script and insert your own name]* We will give the "AskTheCollegeGuy.com Guarantee" that almost everyone you introduce yourself to in those first few days/weeks (assuming they're also new to campus) is going to be just as eager to meet you as you are to meet them – unless you smell funny.

Start meeting people ASAP! If you wait too long, people will already start to have established their circle of friends, they won't be as eager to meet new people, and it will be MUCH harder to get out of your rut and make friends. It won't be impossible, but it will require much more effort on your part.

We realize you probably haven't taken an Economics class yet, but it's simple "Supply And Demand." First day of school, nobody has friends yet (supply of friends is low, demand for friends is high). After a month or so, everyone has their group of friends (supply of friends is high, demand for new friends is low).

2) Open Door Policy - If you live in a dorm with other freshman, DO NOT CLOSE YOUR DOOR unless you're getting dressed or going to sleep (or masturbating). With an open door, you're able to see people walking by -- and say "hi" (if you're girl) or give a head-nod and say "what's up" (if you're a guy). Other people on your hall who are bored or looking to meet new people will stop by to introduce themselves or to see what you're up to if you're door is open, but even the most self-confident of new freshmen isn't likely to knock on a closed door just to say "hey".

Additionally, with an open door, you're able to hear into the hallway if a group is getting ready to go to lunch or order a pizza or go to the gym and you can pop your head into the hall to join them. And above all else, if your door is open you'll be able to see all the hotties from the second floor as they walk by - not that you'll muster the courage to do anything about it in your sad, pathetic, homesick state of mind, but they're still nice to look at anyway.

3) Gettin' Busy - Sign up for different activities and organizations (or at least go to the introductory new members meetings to find out what's out there). Activities and organizations are an easy way to meet new people - and if someone is at the same meeting as you, then you've already got something in common and a conversation starter next time you see them. Wallowing in your self-pity is probably easier than facing the challenge of the unknown. But stop being such a wuss [that's a gender-neutral derogatory term], and get yourself out there. You have to completely submerse yourself into this new experience until you're too damn busy to think about the comforts of home. There's everything from fraternities and sororities to political groups and religious groups, from music and theatre to sports and recreation, from academic clubs or service organizations to student government or the school newspaper - you really have no excuse for your homesickness if you don't get involved in at least something!

And if you can't find an organization you like, start your own. We recommend you start an organization called "Fans of AskTheCollegeGuy.com Celebrating the Kings of Mesmerizing Entertainment." And if that's too long a name, you could shorten it to the acronym "FACK-ME". Imagine the sense of pride you'll have when somebody asks you what organization you belong to and you respond: "FACK ME!"

                                                    -- The College Guy

P.S. IMPORTANT NOTE #1: No matter how homesick you get, do NOT, under any circumstance - unless there is a family emergency - actually go home. When you get back, you'll feel like even more of an outsider than when you left because everyone else will have started forming bonds and friendships that you weren't around to be a part of.

P.S. IMPORTANT NOTE #2: Most of the above applies to both guys and girls who are homesick. Although we have to stress a few things to the guys. The whole "cuddling with a childhood stuffed animal" thing probably won't go over so well with your new roommate. And just be careful with whom you choose to pour your heart out to and share your feelings and emotions with - or the name-sign on your door might be edited to read "Sissy-Boy" or "Pansy-Ass". The sensitive-male thing will only get you so far with the college girls.

[Editors' Note]
In response to those who have written us recently asking if we were serious about the chicken that lived for 18 months without a head...YES! We swear, to The Inventor Of Beer (which is the closest thing to a non-denominational God we could think of), that the story about "Mike The Headless Chicken" is completely true. And speaking of dead fowl, today we're going to kill two birds with one stone.

But before we do that, can we talk about that expression for a minute? Without thinking much about it, most people understand that "to kill two birds with one stone" means to efficiently accomplish two things with the effort, energy, or resources normally reserved for just one thing. But most idiomatic expressions have some literal, reality-based origin - so please think about this particular expression and then tell us who the hell these brutally ruthless savages are out there who are trying to kill birds with rocks?

Seriously, who the hell is so pissed off at the world that they're taking out their anger and frustrations by trying to kill birds with stones?!?! And wouldn't PETA (People for the Ethical Treatment of Animals) be all over their bird-killing asses faster than fraternity guys all over freshmen girls in the first week of school? Not to mention that logistically it would probably take an arm with the strength and accuracy of a big-league pitcher to accomplish such a precise, albeit inhumane, feat. Randy Johnson once killed a bird with a baseball. So maybe it's Curt Schilling or Pedro Martinez who are trying to one-up the Big Unit by going for two birds.

Ok, sorry about all that. We'll make a concerted effort to avoid such ridiculous tangents in the future. [**Editors' Note within an Editors' Note:** No, we will actually make no such effort. If you don't like our tangents, go read something else.] *But for now, we'll get back to the column and we're going to attempt to "kill many birds with 1 stone" by answering several different questions with one all-encompassing answer:*

- ✓ One question from a junior at Oklahoma State complaining of being "bored at school"
- ✓ One question from a sophomore at Ball State saying "there's never anything to do"
- ✓ Multiple questions from multiple students at multiple schools who are homesick
- ✓ One question from a freshman at UNLV who asks "is there anything else to do besides drink?"
- ✓ One question from an anonymous male student at an undisclosed school in Texas who asks "how can I ask a girl out [on a date] if I don't have a car?"

One good, cheap, easily-accessible, universal solution to all of the above problems and situations is... "Addiction!"

Nothing to do on campus? Bored? No car to take a date somewhere? Looking for a weekly "thing" to do with "the guys" or "the girls"? Need some way to take your mind off studying, homesickness, or anything else? Allow yourself to get passionately addicted (no, not to crack) to something on television and then make it a weekly social experience.

We're not saying you should spend every waking hour in front of the TV until you become a huge fat-ass and the pizza delivery guy becomes your best friend, but pick one or two things to start watching on a regular basis, allow yourself to become a true fan, and you'll be hooked before you know it. In addition to the entertainment value, you'll find that having some kind of regular "can't miss" show or televised event can serve all of the following purposes:

- ✓ **stress relief**
- ✓ **boredom relief**
- ✓ **study break**
- ✓ **date night** (hanging out, likely leading to hooking up later)
- ✓ *pseudo*-**date night** (the "hanging out" part, without the "hooking up" part, resulting in at least one of you leaving completely sexually-frustrated)
- ✓ **"guys' night" activity** (a.k.a. "male bonding night")
- ✓ **"girls' night" activity** (a.k.a. "male-bashing night")

Obviously the shows/events that are best-suited to get you completely hooked and serve one or all of the above purposes will vary based on the time of year, but two of the most addictive things on television these days are Reality TV and Sports. So here are 5 suggestions for you to immediately start following (and be sure to watch with other people because if you're passionately addicted to anything by yourself - other than masturbation - you quickly become "the reclusive, introverted, weirdo" that everyone makes fun of).

SPORTS:

It doesn't matter if you're a walking sports almanac who can rattle off Albert Pujol's lifetime batting average, Tom Brady's quarterback rating, and Kevin Garnett's shooting percentage. It doesn't matter if you've never been much of a sports fan at all (although we're hoping you can figure out how many points a 3-pointer is worth in basketball or a 2-point conversion is worth in football). Depending on the time of year, there is almost always a new season starting or a round of playoffs beginning in one sport or another.

1. **Major League Baseball.** No question about it, a 162-game season is way too long for anybody except the most diehard fans to follow closely. But the rest of the world starts to take notice once playoff time rolls around and, if you've got some rooting interest in one of the teams, baseball's post-season can be quite enjoyable, intense, and heart-breaking. Non-baseball fans can arbitrarily pick a team and hop on a bandwagon each September/October. NOTE: Under no circumstance should bandwagon fans pretend to know more or to be a better fan than the diehards who have been following the team for years - it's just not cool and the real fans will definitely want to kick your ass.

2. **Football (college OR pro).** Whether you're at a sports bar, someone's apartment, or a dorm room down the hall, watching football is probably one of the easiest ways to bond and make friends. And girls, don't think for a minute that this is only a male-bonding thing; there are very few things in this world that are cooler to a guy than a girl who likes to throw down a few beers while watching football. *[Editors' Note To All The Girls Out There: No matter what the guys tell you, BJ's at halftime are not football-viewing requirements... but topless third quarters are mandatory.]*

3. The start of your academic year coincides with the starts of both the college and pro seasons, so it's a

perfect time to become a football fan (just be aware that this is different than the intramural games at your school - this is "tackle football" so if you yell "Pull his flag! Pull his flag!" you're going to look like a moron).

4. **March Madness.** If you don't know what March Madness is then you need to go directly to NASA and tell them what it's been like living on another planet for so long. Anyway, as Dick Vitale will tell you, the NCAA hoops tournament is "awesome, baby!" And it's infinitely awesomer* if you happen to be lucky enough to attend one of the 64 schools playing in the tourney (65 if you count that stupid-ass play-in game; seriously can anybody explain the logic behind that? Let's see, we've got a perfectly symmetrical tournament bracket, but let's add one more team, one more game, and really screw things up just for fun, just because we can, just because we have that power. Absolutely absurd.)

[Editors' Note: Yes, we know "awesomer" isn't really a word. We just put it in there for fun, just because we can, just because we have that power – Hey, NCAA Tournament Committee, doesn't make any sense, does it?]

REALITY TV:

Talk about jumping on a bandwagon, it seems like every other show on TV these days is "Reality TV," but don't be fooled by the bitter skeptics who say "Reality TV is all a bunch of trashy crap." While there is certainly some Reality-crap out there, some of it is still damn entertaining - and addictive. It doesn't matter if you're a Reality-TV-Virgin, or if you're a Reality-TV-Slut who can name every Real World cast member from the past 12 years, we suggest tuning in to the latest season of Survivor (CBS), The Apprentice (NBC),

The Bachelor/Bachelorette (ABC), or whatever FOX comes up with next (*Who Wants to Marry My Big Fat Obnoxious Midget Dad Named Joe Idol?*). Anyway, check your local listings and allow yourself to get addicted!

In addition to most of the above being fun for entertainment purposes, they also give you something to bet on with friends (not that we can go on the record to condone illegal gambling, but...). You can probably already figure out how to bet on sports, but Reality TV is fun to gamble on too:

- ✓ Choose the Survivor contestant you think will outwit (manipulate and backstab), outplay (eat the nastiest sh*t), and outlast (end up 25 pounds lighter, covered in mosquito bites, and on the verge of a mental breakdown).

- ✓ Pick the Bachelor/Bachelorette contestant whose past will come back to haunt them in the form of an internet-circulated porn video.

Anyway, we'll stop there. Enjoy your television-watching, good luck getting addicted, and we accept no responsibility for any adverse effects that our suggestions may have on your health or GPA.

--The College Guy

Chapter Two
-OCTOBER-

QUESTION:
What up College Guy,
I'm having a really tough time making it to my 8:00 class every morning. It really sucks. Any suggestions?
                -- Chris, a sleep-deprived freshman at UT

ANSWER:
What up Chris,

Sure, we've got a suggestion for you: DON'T TAKE 8:00 CLASSES!

We were thinking about giving this advice over the summer or during the first week of the semester when freshmen still had a chance to adjust their schedules to avoid the dreaded early morning classes. But instead we decided to be dicks and wait until October, when it was already too late for Chris and all the other freshmen out there. But don't be mad at us. Instead, think of the hell you experience every morning at 8:00 as a rite of passage or an initiation of sorts.

Very few first-semester freshmen realize just how different "college time" is from "high school time." For years and years, students just like you have been making the mistake of thinking "well, I got up even earlier than this in high school, so early morning college classes won't be so bad." And it's not until it's too late to change your schedule that you realize just how wrong you were and just how much your early morning classes are going to suck.

It doesn't matter how early Mommy or Daddy got you out of bed for high school. College is different. You're living with your friends, there's always something to do, and you're likely missing out on fun (or at least a pepperoni pizza) by going to bed early. So those early morning classes in college tend to seem MUCH earlier than they did in high school.

And since the unofficial weekend begins on Thursdays at many colleges, your early classes on Fridays can be twice as miserable and they often lead to a difficult dilemma: Stumble into class, hung-over, smelling like beer, and sporting a vomit-stained T-shirt? Or just stay in bed and skip the class completely? Unless you're hooking up with your Professor or your T.A., your grade in the class is probably going to suffer either way.

-- The College Guy

P.S. There are some students reading this who will completely disagree with us and won't be able to relate to our response to this question at all. These are the (weird) students who actually enjoy early classes. These are the (weird) students that will continue to take the 8:00 and 8:30 classes every semester until graduation. And of course, these are the (weird) students who will probably end up as the future leaders of the world.

But Chris and all the other (normal) students out there (who actually have fun in college and want to smash their alarm clocks every morning) are the ones who will quickly learn to schedule nothing but afternoon classes. But don't worry; slack-asses have a future too. You'll either be the future toilet-scrubbers of the world or the future humor/advice columnists of the world like us!

QUESTION:
What's the big deal about going to the library? Everybody's always going to the library but I personally don't see any problem studying in my room.
-- Studying in the Dorm, Bucknell

ANSWER:
Oh, you poor deprived soul....
The college library phenomenon is unlike anything else you will find in any environment or living situation anywhere in the world for the rest of your life! While the particular dynamics of each university's library will vary slightly from campus to campus, there are a few factors which remain constant. The most notable of these common threads are: WHO is there and WHY they are there.

- ✓ Some students go to the library for the sole purpose of doing work (after all, if we paid attention during College Orientation, that is what we were taught the library is for). These students either need the library's resources (to do research, find books, or use the library's computers) or they just find it to be a good place to read, study, or write papers away from roommates and the craziness and distractions of dorms or apartments.

- ✓ Some students go to the library for the sole purpose of socializing, seeing friends, trying to find a date, etc. These students appreciate the library's ***other*** resources, namely the other students who are there. If you think about it, the library is really a perfect place to try to meet somebody. What's the hardest part about trying to meet a new guy or girl? As Adam Sandler told his kid in Big Daddy, "Initiating the conversation is half the battle." And when you're at the library you've automatically got something in common to talk about. Even if you're studying Philosophy and the hot sophomore on your left is studying Biology, you're both at the library, (supposedly) studying, and that's enough for even the most socially awkward person to start a conversation with: "Test tomorrow?" or "So is that Bio class as hard as I've heard it is?" Whatever. The actual line doesn't matter - you've initiated the conversation.

Plus, if it goes OK, you've got the added bonus of now having an opening line the next time you see him or her on campus or out at a party: "Hey, so how did that Biology mid-term go that you were studying for the other night?" Bam! You're in!!!

✓ Some students go to the library because it offers the perfect combination of the two scenarios described above (academic vs. social). You've got a place where you can at least attempt to get the work done that you have to do, but at the same time you've got plenty of people to see and talk to if you want to get up and walk around for a little "study break." Be warned, if you choose to use the library for both academic and social purposes, you may find that the social appeal outweighs the academic benefits and you might not get much work done even though you're "going to the library" every night. Well, you'll hopefully be getting work done either way, but your "work" might consist of flirting and getting phone numbers.

           -- The College Guy

QUESTION:
Right now I am a freshman and I have met probably one of the nicest and non-fake girl I have ever met. The problem is she has a boyfriend back in her home state. I have known her for about 2 months and we hang out at least three times a week and talk everyday like best friends. Anyways could you give me any tips on getting her?

           -- Freshman In Love, Ole Miss

ANSWER:
So you've met the girl of your dreams but, WTF, she's already taken? Well gosh golly gee who would'a thunk it? *(Mock surprise on our part)* A girl as great as the one you describe and she's already got a guy? Damn it! Why are the good ones always taken? The way we see it, you've basically got three options:

Option #1: Just Be Patient

> *I've met this girl I want to date.*
> *She's frickin' perfect; I think it's fate.*
> *Good things come to those who wait.*
> *So I'll bide my time and masturbate.*

Be the best friend for now and wait for your opportunity. Get close to her in way that no one else can. Earn her trust. Be there for her when she has the fight with her roommate or when her grandmother dies. [Note: Don't be the one that actually causes the fight between her and her roommate and definitely don't be the one that actually kills her grandmother – or at least don't get caught!] Basically, get her to fall in love with you without her realizing that she's falling in love with you. The goal of this strategy is that she'll realize she's in love with you immediately upon breaking up with him – or she'll realize she's in love with you and that will actually be a catalyst for her breaking it off with him.

DISCLAIMER: The "Patience" strategy can backfire in a few different ways:

Patience Backfire #1: She beats the odds and stays with the boyfriend leaving you eternally frustrated as the poor, pathetically patient, platonic friend.

Patience Backfire #2: She does end up breaking up with her dude, but it's because she fell for some *other* guy at your school (possibly beginning with a random, drunken hookup -- that sneaky bastard!) and just like that, she's moved from Guy #1 to Guy #3, leaving you (Guy #2) with no chance to work your mojo and make the leap from best friend to boyfriend.

Option #2: Tell Her Without Actually "Telling" Her

You like her so much, these situations suck.
You'd rather be run over by a huge-ass truck.
So <u>subtly</u> tell her, and with a little luck,
You and she will one day... [date?]

Let her know how you feel, but do it *very subtly*. Ideally this would come after you've developed the close friendship described above so she trusts you and cares about you on some relatively deep level.

When she wants to vent about her boyfriend for the hundredth time, do NOT try to convince her to break up with him. She will end up resenting you for it and she'll immediately question your motives. If it's been a while and you two are really at the super-close, best-friends level, you can make a subtle move by saying something like: "Listen, if you need me to be here for you so you can talk about your boyfriend issues, I guess I can do that because I care about you. But I really don't think it should be *me* actually giving you advice on the situation..."

And say no more.

She'll ask you what you mean by that, but there's no need to elaborate. A simple "never mind, forget it" should suffice to get you out of the conversation. But you've done what you intended to do. You've subtly, without making her uncomfortable, put the idea in her head that you might like her a little more than the "just friends" thing. But hopefully she'll respect the fact that you haven't tried to make a move or profess your love while she's in a relationship. But nonetheless, you've started the wheels turning in her head.

If the above dialogue doesn't fit your style, there are several other ways to subtly get your feelings across:

✓ Each time the boyfriend's name comes up, go from your normal fun, personable self to a slightly sadder, "my dog just got hit by a tractor" kind of demeanor. Don't over-exaggerate this or you'll look like a psycho, but just enough of an attitude change to get her or one of her friends to notice. But again, if they ask what's wrong, do the whole "What? Oh, it's nothing, no big deal" kind of reaction.

✓ "Accidentally" let something out when you're drinking. Be careful with this tactic because you don't want it to develop into a long drunken discussion or argument. But say just enough so she takes notice. The next day you can either pretend you don't remember or you can say something like "Hey, if I said anything last night that was inappropriate, I'm really sorry. I know you've got a boyfriend and I didn't mean to...."

✓ Reluctantly confide in one of her friends - ideally one of her friends who likes you more than she likes the other guy. Preface it with something like "Ok, but you have to promise not to tell anyone…" Your girl is guaranteed to hear every word of your "secret feelings" within 24 hours. Oh, the power of girl-gossip.

Option #3: All Or Nothing – Just Tell Her!

> *I'm not patient enough to "wait and see,"*
> *And those Jedi-mind games aren't for me.*
> *I'm just gonna tell her and then we'll see.*
> *If she dumps that douche-bag and gets with me.*

Tired of being the platonic close friend? Don't feel like "wasting" time just being friends or playing the aforementioned games? Just be careful, because once you lay your feelings on the line like that, it becomes nearly impossible to go back to what you had before.

Worst Case Scenario - Her reaction: *"What the hell??!!?? So all this time you only hung out with me because you've been hoping I'd break up with [boyfriend]. You knew I was in a relationship! You knew I just wanted to be friends* *with you! I thought of you like a brother! But now, I don't even know if I want to be in the same room as you! Wait 'til [boyfriend] finds out about this. He's gonna kick your ass. Get out! I don't even want to look at you!"*

Best Case Scenario - Her reaction: *"Wow! I had no idea. Part of why I was staying with [soon-to-be-EX-boyfriend] is because I didn't think I would find anybody else. I've actually been thinking about you like that for a while now. I just didn't think you felt the same way so I didn't want to risk our friendship by saying anything about how I felt. I've been thinking about breaking up with him for a while now, but I was afraid to be alone. Give me a little time to figure all this out, but I'm really glad you decided to tell me about this."* In a perfect world, she'll say all this while holding your hand and looking deep into your eyes.

Final Recap: Whether you wait it out, drop subtle hints, or just go for it, we wish you all the best! Keep us posted.

            -- The College Guy

QUESTION:
I didn't get into the sorority I wanted to and I'm a mess.

            -- Ali, IU

ANSWER:
It's a good thing Alex Trebek isn't on our staff because your response was definitely not in the form of a question. Sometimes when we get e-mails like that (without an actual question), we send back a wiseass response with a dictionary definition of the word "question" attached. But in this case we'll just try to figure out what the "intended question" might have been:

A. I didn't get into the sorority I wanted to and I'm a mess, so should I transfer?
B. I didn't get into the sorority I wanted to and I'm a mess, so will my friends still talk to me?
C. I didn't get into the sorority I wanted to and I'm a mess, so is there something wrong with me?
D. I didn't get into the sorority I wanted to and I'm a mess so do you think a vibrator would help?
E. I didn't get into the sorority I wanted to and I'm a mess so can you just comment on that general situation for me?

ANSWERS:

A. No
B. Yes
C. No
D. Maybe
E. OK, here we go...

Fraternities and Sororities can be a great thing for college students, and at different schools they play drastically different roles in the campus social scene (the dominating social outlet at some schools and virtually non-existent at other schools). But there is NO college where it should ever be considered the literal end of the world if you don't get into a fraternity or sorority (or if you don't get in to the specific one of your choice).

Certainly there are some Greek systems where being non-Greek will make things more difficult for you socially, but all that means is that you'll have to put in a little more effort once you get over your initial shock, disappointment, embarrassment, devastation, or whatever other emotions you may experience.

✓ You might have to actively seek out groups, clubs, teams, or activities to get involved with because you won't have a fraternity or sorority to keep you busy.

✓ You might have to make a few additional phone calls when you want to get a group together to go out at night.

✓ You might have to make more of an effort to keep in touch with your friends that will be busy pledging their fraternity or sorority.

✓ You might have to be proactive and introduce yourself to a few more people to make some more friends because you won't automatically have that group of 20, 50, or 100+ guys or girls that will automatically be your "brothers" or "sisters".

BUT, as long as you don't roll over and accept/assume that your life is going to suck because you didn't get the bid you wanted, you will end up just fine, even if it seems like everyone you know is pledging. Just pull yourself together emotionally, accept the fact that you'll have to put in some extra effort to keep yourself busy and to keep yourself happy socially. If you're able to do this, then you'll end up with just as good a chance of having a great college experience as all your other friends (even the ones that will be carrying around a paddle, eating dog food, doing elephant walks, or any number of other things that never happen because they're outlawed by national hazing policies).

-- The College Guy

QUESTION:
Why is it more likely that college freshmen will fail out than college sophomores or juniors or seniors?

-- Jennifer, Eastern Michigan University

ANSWER:

A recently conducted AskTheCollegeGuy.com survey showed that 75% of college students agree that freshmen are the dumbest of all college students. *[Note: That 75%, of course, is comprised entirely of sophomores, juniors, and seniors.]*

Quite simply, many freshmen are not accustomed to the freedom that comes with college. And, at the risk of sounding like your mother (something which makes us want to kick our own collective AskTheCollegeGuy.com ass), with that new freedom comes great responsibility. *[Editors' Note: That line either sounds familiar because you actually heard it from your parents, or because it's pretty damn close to Peter Parker's "With great power comes great responsibility" in Spiderman.]*

Many freshmen, who are away from home for the first time, in an environment that encourages drinking, includes no parental supervision, and allows you to schedule all your classes after noon if you want to, are -- somewhat justifiably -- unable to adjust. Finding the balance between work and play can be tough. But, by the time a college student reaches sophomore year, two things have happened...

1.   Most of the college students who were destined to fail out have already done so (and if you've already failed out as a freshman, you are likely back at home with Ma and Pa - therefore taking you out of the running to become a sophomore-, junior-, or senior-flunk-out).

2.   You've got at least a year of college experience and personal growth under your belt (of course, your belt likely makes a larger circle these days after the 'freshman fifteen') and you've already learned what works and what doesn't work, what you can get

away with and what you can't get away with, and you've likely been a little wiser about picking your classes compared to your clueless class selections of freshman year. Juggling the temptations of partying with the necessary study-time has likely gotten easier too - even fun if your study group decides to try shotgunning beers while cramming for that final. Regardless, upperclassmen have been there, done that, and learned from "the freshman experience".

-- The College Guy

QUESTION:
I've heard it said that most girls fake orgasms, so how do I make sure I give my girlfriend an orgasm?

-- Wants to Please Her, USC

ANSWER:
We could dive into detailed, sexually-explicit conversation about the clitoris, the g-spot, and everything else down there that may or may not constitute foreign, uncharted territory to many guys out there. But we can do one better than that.

We our going to give you the one universal technique that we guarantee will work with more women than any other orgasm-inducing technique out there. This patented, top-secret technique will undoubtedly give you the best possible chance of successfully bringing your girlfriend to orgasm and becoming the master of your sexual destiny.

You have absolutely just taken a step in the right direction. You've acknowledged that you might not necessarily know exactly what you're doing down there... and you've asked for help. Good for you; give yourself a pat on the back.

Anyway, the only problem with asking The College Guy how to give your girlfriend and orgasm is that we've never hooked up *with her* so we don't know exactly what does it *for her* (or maybe we *have* hooked up with her, we *do* know what does it for her, we *have* given her earth-shattering, mind-numbing orgasms, and we're just playing dumb so you don't catch on that we've been nailing your girl... hmmmm).

Anyway, the point is that the only person who can give you the secret to getting your girlfriend to orgasm is your girlfriend herself... so all you have to do is ... (drum roll, please) ... ASK HER!

That's it! So simple. Ask her what she likes and what she doesn't. Ask her what feels good and what doesn't. Let her know that you really want to give her an orgasm and ask her to help you by teaching you what works for her.

This may seem too simple and you might even call it a cop-out answer... but believe us, it works. Earn her trust, show her you care, and then let *her* guide you to your goal... and if you get really good, she might even brag to her friends about you!

The College Guy

QUESTION:
My roommate is really getting on my nerves. She makes a lot of noise in the morning, listens to her music on surround sound, and leaves the door open while I'm half naked. I'll say something, only to have her comply for about 10 minutes before she starts again. What should I do?

-- Annoyed Roommate,
University of Northern Colorado

ANSWER:

Did you say half-naked?!? So, um, what do you look like? ...Ok, sorry about that.

First of all, don't just say "something" in passing -- have a real conversation about it. It is totally appropriate to request a sit-down with a roommate if there's a conflict, whether it be scheduling, (she might have early classes, while you have late classes), music issues (anything from genre to volume), or nakedness (maybe she grew up in a nudist colony so she is unaware of your bashfully modest need to keep the whole dorm from checking out your boobs and tan lines).

By virtue of the fact that you're writing us instead of talking to her, it appears you might not be the most confrontational person on the planet. Only child perhaps? But anyway, you've got to confront your roommate about what's bothering you or it's only going to get worse. Here are some tips in case the idea of initiating this conversation excites you as much as the idea of playing leap-frog with unicorns *[Editors' Note: Yes, we took that line from the Rejection Hotline message, but we know the guy, so it's cool.]*

✓ Do not, under any circumstance, begin to yell at her. You'll look like an ass, you'll solidify your roommate relationship as unpleasantly hostile for the rest of the year, and she will be adamant about continuing the exact things you wanted her to stop doing.

✓ On the flip side, don't let her walk all over you either. Be firm and clear as you explain what bothers you and why. Tell her the exact things that need to be worked on and be sure to have a list of specific incidents in case she tells you that you're full of shit. *[Editors' Note: If you think there is any chance of this conversation escalating into a hair-pulling cat-fight, be sure to set up a video camera to get the whole thing on tape -- and you'd damn well better send an unedited copy to AskTheCollegeGuy.com Headquarters.]*

✓ Offer to compromise. If you say that you understand that it's hard to adjust to living with someone new and give an example of something that you plan on changing to suit her needs (maybe she hates the fact that you never do laundry and the room smells funky because of your dirty socks) she will be far more willing to admit that she needs to concede some bad habits too.

The big thing to remember about any roommate conflict is that it rarely does any good to bitch, moan, and complain about it. Talk to your roommate, open up the lines of communication, and most of the time you can improve the situation without the use of semi-automatic weapons.

If you try all of the above and the situation is still unbearable, just remember: unlike herpes, it is possible to get rid of a roommate. Talk to your RA and see about room transfer options. Just be sure your current situation is really as bad as you think it is, because things can always get worse -- just imagine your new roommate being a 600-pound, belly-dancing, trombone-playing, Jehovah's Witness who suffers from nasty body odor, bad breath, and Chronic Flatulence Syndrome, just joined the school yodeling team, and has a pet python named Sneaky Stevie.

-- ***The College Guy***

Chapter Three
-NOVEMBER-

QUESTION:
My boyfriend was away at college for 3 months and he hasn't called me or written me. Please help.
                                    -- BabyGirl, Still in High School

ANSWER:
So your boyfriend hasn't called you in 3 months? Um, BabyGirl, we hate to be the bearer of bad news (actually, that's not true, we really enjoy it), but he's NOT your boyfriend anymore (assuming he ever was). Unless he's lying in a ditch somewhere, it's a safe bet that he's moved on and you should too. Very sorry about that. But don't be too upset; there's good news too... we just saved $100 by switching to Geiko!
                                              --The College Guy

QUESTION:
Whenever I come home from school for Thanksgiving, Christmas, or any other break, my parents want to know each night where I'm going, who I'm going with, and when I'll be home. It's so annoying since when I'm away at school, I can do whatever I want.
                                              -- Alex, UK

ANSWER:

Hopefully you've figured this out from talking to your friends, but this is definitely not a situation unique to you and your parents. While some parents are more lenient/trusting/fair/cool than others, there are many families across the country that struggle with issues of control/freedom/rules over the summers and other college breaks.

Just so we can say that we have at least tried to see both sides of this issue, we will address the viewpoints of *both* the college student *and* the parent (so this response might get a little long and rambling, but we don't really care since you didn't actually ask a question -- look above for yourself, there's no real question, just a frustrated rant).

The Parents' Viewpoint

*[Editors' Note: Don't take this to mean we're on your parents' side here (because we definitely understand the frustration of going from the absolute freedom of college life to the curfews and whatever other rules your parents try to enforce while you're at home), but it really does help to at least **try** to see where the other side is coming from.]*

Most parents pay the college tuition and support their college student financially and all they really want while you're home for break is a little bit of courtesy, respect, and to know what you're doing. Yes, that's *very* different from the absolute freedom you are accustomed to at college, but your parents probably don't want to accept or even acknowledge those freedoms you have at school. Much like you don't ever want to think about the idea of your parents ever having had sex (even though you probably have some idea of how you and any siblings were conceived), similarly your parents don't want to acknowledge the possibility that you can drink, smoke, and have sex, basically whenever you want to at college. They are your parents and they still want to feel as though they have some control over their little boy or girl.

By fighting them on all their rules, you deny them what they perceive as this parental right and they feel disrespected at the same time. And whether you can admit it or not, you know that most of the questions and rules that your mom and dad bombard you with are really only hurled at you because they care about you, worry about you, and want what's best for you. Ok, sorry, enough with the sentimental, tear-jerking, after-school-special crap. Let's get back to why the loss of freedom pisses you off so much.

The Student's Viewpoint
[Note: Since there aren't too many parents that read this column, the college student will most likely have to convey this message to his or her parents. But we highly suggest you don't do so in the yelling, screaming, argumentative, "I'm right; you're wrong" kind of way. The reason that never works is because you undermine their parental authority when you openly challenge them -- and that's the worst possible way to try to get them to see your point of view – even when you KNOW you're right.]

OK, so we probably don't really need to explain the college student viewpoint because you already know how you feel: Away at school, you can do whatever you want whenever you want with whomever you want with minimal rules - and then suddenly, back at home, you have rules, curfews, and parents to answer to again... and your freedom is suddenly ripped away from you – leaving you to feel kinda like Mel Gibson in BraveHeart – and it SUCKS).

But rather than fighting with your parents about it, try having a real, adult conversation with them to explain your point of view. For starters it may impress them that you're handling things in a mature and rational manner and they may start to see that college is changing their little boy or girl into a responsible adult (little do they need to know about skipped classes, keg stands, bong hits, or late-night booty calls). If you initiate the conversation and/or make a suggestion that involves the word "compromise", they might very well fall over in shock.

If rational conversation doesn't work, one technique that can occasionally be effective (though you should feel guilty as hell for playing this card) is to explain – again, calmly and rationally – that if you have all this freedom at college and no freedom at home then you might not want to spend your future summers and holiday breaks at home anymore. You might subtly ask them if these rules and their need for control are so important to them that they would really rather drive you away forever rather than be willing to compromise and accept the fact that you're not such a little kid anymore. *[Note: This guilt trip approach only works if your parents actually like you. Otherwise, if they think of you as an annoying little shit whom they can't wait to get rid of, they might not really care if you threaten to never come back.]*

The bottom line is that you should try to explain your position as calmly and rationally as possible without disrespecting your parents, challenging their authority, or seeming unappreciative of the fact that they pay your tuition. Ideally you want to help them see that the same rules they applied to you when you were a 16-year-old High Schooler might not necessarily be the best rules for you now that you are an older, more mature and responsible college student.

Of course, if all else fails and the rational/diplomatic approach is unsuccessful, you could always just do what comes naturally – throw a temper tantrum, tell them to go to hell, ignore all their rules, and sneak out with your friends anyway. What were we saying about "more mature and responsible"?

The College Guy

QUESTION:
I'm not really happy here at school so I'm thinking of transferring, but everybody I talk to tells me what a horrible idea it is. What's so bad about transferring?

-- Time to Transfer, unnamed college

ANSWER:
Sometimes there's nothing wrong with transferring... but other times, it's as good an idea as letting a kid have a sleep-over at Michael Jackson's ranch.

Too many people make the mistake of associating their unhappiness at college with the particular school itself. If you haven't made any friends, if you're not doing well in the classroom, or if you're not enjoying yourself, what makes you think it will be any different at a new school???

Regardless of which college you attend, you're going to have to make an effort to meet people, to study, and to get involved on campus. Every freshman dorm (at every college or university) has plenty of kids who sit around in their room unhappy, many talking about transferring. The reality of the situation is that many haven't done a damn thing to first try to improve their existing situation at their current school.

Unless there is a concrete reason, specifically associated with the college you currently attend, we think transferring because you're "not happy" is a terrible idea. Change the things about yourself that are keeping you from being happy, don't switch schools.

COLLEGE GUY FACT: The vast majority of college students who transfer for social reasons end up being just as unhappy at their new school.

All of the above not withstanding, there are certain situations in which transferring can be a good decision for a college student. Some such situations include:

Financial Reasons:

- ✓ Acceptable: You can't afford the school you're currently at so you need to transfer to a less expensive school.
- ✓ Acceptable: You initially couldn't afford the school you wanted to attend, but through scholarships, inheritance, a successful bank robbery, or some other stroke of luck, you can now afford your first choice.
- ✓ **Un**acceptable: You spend too much money on alcohol so you need to transfer to a college in a state like New Hampshire where it's cheaper.

Academic Reasons:

- ✓ Acceptable: You've tried, but you simply can't handle the academic load at your current school so you need to transfer to a school with a slightly less rigorous academic program. *[Note: That's the politically correct way of saying "you're a dumbass who's flunking out"]*
- ✓ Acceptable: For whatever the reason you are now a better applicant for a school with a significantly better academic reputation (i.e. you started at East Oshkosh Horticultural Community College and for some reason you can now get into and/or afford to pay tuition at a higher- caliber school that would be better for your future.)

✓ Acceptable: Your current school doesn't have the academic program you are looking for or you would be better suited with your particular field of study in another part of the country/world *[Note: Do not transfer to Latin America to study Latin).*

✓ **Un**acceptable: "Like, dude, my buddy said they don't have classes on Arbor Day at his school! I'm definitely transferin' there!"

> *-- The College Guy*

QUESTION:

I go to a small private Southern Baptist college. When we have members of the opposite sex in our room we have to leave the door open, light on, and are patrolled by the Dorm Nazis every fifteen minutes. The "parking" spots are all known and patrolled by cops because it is a horrendously small town. The local park closes at midnight and is also patrolled by cops. If you get caught in a compromising situation you can pretty much count on getting expelled because of a student code of conduct we were required to sign. Oh yeah, this is a dry county too - so no alcohol or big parties. And to top it all off, my significant other and I are only 19 and 20. So we can't get a room at most hotels just to spend some time together. Where can we go to make out, pet, etc.? I don't care about having sex, I just need to release some of this energy. Help!

> *-- Dying from pent up sexual energy,*
> *An unnamed private Southern Baptist college*

ANSWER:

Yep, this does sound like quite a piteous predicament. Our first thought is "Why the hell are you going to this school in the first place?!" What kind of college is this? Dry county? Curfews? No parties? No sex? We had more fun in Kindergarten!

[Editors' Note: In response to the obnoxious jackasses who have written us complaining that this implies that we condone alcohol consumption and sex for Kindergartners -- it was merely exaggeration to emphasize a point, hyperbole if you will... so shut up, get a life, and either keep reading or start your own website at OverSensitiveReaders.com, but don't waste our time.]

Ok, here are 3 options for you (the respective pros and cons of which should be self-explanatory):

1. Suck it up and pray that your time until graduation passes by quickly.
2. Resort to *(and hope to quickly move from novice to expert in)* the art of self-pleasure.
3. Or, you could take the "Screw That!" approach and get the hell out of there! Get yourself into the most compromising position you could possibly be found in... and *let yourself get caught.*

[Editors' Note: If you take this approach, PLEASE contact us and let us know how it turns out... Extra Points will be awarded if your compromising situation of choice involves barnyard animals, chocolate syrup, and a pregnant midget.]

With any luck, they'll throw your horny, sex-deprived asses right out of that ridiculous, tight-ass University of Suck and you can attend a real college in the free world where you'll have plenty of opportunities to release some of that sexual energy you've been harboring.

-- *The College Guy*

QUESTION:
I have a difficult time with multiple choice tests. And because this kind of test is a major part of any of my grades, my GPA

is suffering. Do you have any suggestions or advice as to how to approach these kinds of tests in the future?

-- Struggling Steph, Ohio University

ANSWER:

Ok, you're about to get the best advice you'll ever find regarding multiple choice tests. First, as you probably already know (unless you went to Knibb High School with Billy Madison and had teachers like Miss Lippy), a multiple choice question consists of one correct answer and three or four incorrect answers. Now that we're clear on that, listen up, because here comes the advice that Kaplan and Princeton Review only wishes they could give. Our strategy for taking multiple choice tests is ... (drum roll please)... you should ignore the incorrect answers and select the correct answer. Yes, we know, pure genius! And what's even better is that this advice comes with a money-back guarantee. If you select the correct answer and stay away from the incorrect answers, we guarantee you'll start seeing better results on your multiple choice tests and your GPA is sure to improve.

Alright, sorry, that last paragraph might have been written after one too many Beast Lights. We realize that wasn't much of a response to a serious question, so we'll try a little harder in paragraphs three and four.

The truth is that a lot of kids suck at these kinds of tests too, so for starters, don't let it make you feel like a mental midget. Some people are naturally smarter than others and some people are naturally better test-takers than others. It can be the most frustrating thing in the world if you study your ass off for a big test, putting in hours and hours of study time, only to find that your roommate or some random jackass in your class did better than you when you know you studied twice as much as they did.

But 9 times out of 10, when you say you were studying for four hours, how many hours were you really studying? One? Two? Two and a half at most? If you're not going to study the whole time, that's not a problem, it's normal; just don't kid yourself into thinking you studied for four hours when more than half that time was likely spent instant messaging friends (at least one of whom was probably sitting five feet away from you), taking coffee breaks (often times before you even start studying), or playing Beirut (or beer pong, depending on what part of the country you're from).

Anyway, the most important thing - once you actually start studying - is to make sure that you're not just studying, but that you're studying properly and efficiently. Most colleges offer some type of study skills classes or workshops (possibly through a student support services department or whatever a similar department might be called at your school). In most cases, these services are rarely used by even close to the number of students who could benefit from them. Also, in many cases there is no additional cost for taking a study skills class or workshop because it's covered by a student services portion of your tuition. But even if does cost something, it will certainly be worth it to learn how to study properly and to get some test-taking strategies relevant to a specific subject and a specific kind of test. For example, essay and short-answer questions are easier to get through with an understanding of basic concepts and a general understanding of the material, so a reading/studying technique of skimming for main ideas with special attention paid to chapter summaries might be most beneficial. On the flip side, your multiple choice tests are generally more detail-oriented and specific, so being able to explain concepts and B.S. your way through essays doesn't do much for you if you don't know specific names, dates, formulas, calculations, or whatever else your multiple choice questions will be asking for depending on the subject.

If you follow all of the above advice and you're still having trouble, one great way to dodge most forms of tests is to declare an English major (or journalism or creative writing or underwater skydiving). If you start taking more writing-intensive classes, your test-taking struggles are sure to become a thing of the past ... plus iff yu becom a good righter you kan gett kool oportunites like righting four AskTheCollegeGuy.com.

                                    -- The College Guy

P.S. Anyone who writes in to tell us that we messed up because Miss Lippy wasn't a teacher at Knibb High School -- save it! We consider ourselves to be Billy Madison experts (and we are well aware of the fact that Miss Lippy's defining moment was her stirring recitation of The Puppy Who Lost His Way.) Besides, if you're correcting us on that, then you sound like a meticulous, detail-oriented, over-achiever who had no business reading a question about struggles with multiple choice tests - so why don't you just sit your ass down and have a nice warm glass of shut-the-hell-up! (and yes, we know that was Happy Gilmore and not Billy Madison... so why don't you stop nit-picking, go back to our homepage, find another question to read, and leave us the $#&% alone!)

P.P.S. If anyone reading this column has never seen Billy Madison - or Tommy Boy, Ferris Bueller's Day Off, American Pie, and Dazed and Confused for that matter - you are officially banned from this website for the rest of eternity unless/until you go rent them, watch them, and love them. Please report back when you are done and your AskTheCollegeGuy.com reading privileges will be restored. If you choose to disregard these orders, may you die of gonorrhea and rot in hell.

QUESTION:

Hey, I was just wondering what turns a guy on? what makes him want you? where can u touch him to make him horny, I have always wondered that and I can never find the right spot! also, what kind of words/ expressions make them horny!! please w/b thanx!

-- Looking for the secret, Tulsa

ANSWER:

What turns a guy on?!?? Are you serious?

[Editors' Note: Do your friends know you've only been dating gay guys?]

Ok, it can actually be very, very difficult to turn a guy on, so pay attention because you have to know EXACTLY what you're doing.

Lucky for you, AskTheCollegeGuy.com is here to help. We have done our research and the results of our meticulously conducted study show there are exactly 9 ways to turn a guy on.

- ✓ Touching a guy - pretty much *anywhere* on his body - will turn him on.

- ✓ Touching yourself - again, pretty much anywhere on *your* body - will turn him on.

- ✓ Touching one of your friends will turn a guy on.

- ✓ One of your friends touching you will turn a guy on.

- ✓ Just *talking* about touching the guy will turn him on.

✓ Talking about touching *yourself* will turn him on.

✓ Talking about touching *your friend* will turn him on.

✓ Talking about your friend touching anyone who is thinking about talking about touching someone who is talking about someone who is thinking about talking about touching anyone will turn him on.

So the better question is "What *doesn't* turn guys on?" And, of course, the only answer to this is "Grandpa in the shower."

In conclusion, getting a guy horny is only slightly easier than breathing (and that's not meant as an insensitive dig at anyone with asthma). Anything even remotely relating to sex will turn a guy on. Most things that have nothing to do with sex will turn guys on. Seriously, what the hell is wrong with you?

-- *The College Guy*

P.S. What's that? You're a math major and your TI-85 calculated that our list only included 8 ways to turn a guy on and we promised 9? Oh, sorry about that. The 9th thing that will turn a guy on is... PORN!

QUESTION:
I had plans to go to a dance club with my roommate the other night but she bailed because she found out that her dog had died that day. I was pretty pissed that she was being so lame, but whatever, I went out with some other girls on the hall instead. But now it's 2 days later and she's still upset about her stupid dog. She's acting like it was a real person

or something and I want to know why she's being such a freak about it?

-- *Abby, University of Arizona*

ANSWER:
Wow! First of all, we are fighting the temptation to just go off on you and call you a stupid, insensitive, cold-hearted, self-absorbed bitch. But, since that wouldn't be very professional of us, we'll try to restrain ourselves.

We don't want to spend any more time than is absolutely necessary answering your question, so pay attention. You have obviously never been a pet-owner (and if you have, we pity whatever pet you have/had because you have clearly never been a *loving* pet-owner – so we hope it pissed all over your bed, threw-up on your floor, and shit in your shoes).

People who have never loved a pet can sometimes not comprehend how the love for a pet can often be as strong as the love for a person. And trust us when we say that the loss of a long-time family pet can be incredibly difficult and painful. So there is NOTHING abnormal at all about your roommate being upset about her loss -- we'd actually have been surprised if she *had* felt like going out dancing that night (especially with a stupid, insensitive, cold-hearted, self-absorbed bitch like you).

Your roommate will start to be more like herself with a little bit of time, but until that happens, we think you should try to be a little more sympathetic to what she's going through. And we're sure if you ask some of your other friends what they think about the situation (assuming you have other friends), you'll be shocked to see that most will understand and sympathize with what your roommate is going through.

-- *The College Guy*

Chapter Four
-DECEMBER-

QUESTION:
Dear College Guy,
What is a toga party? Do people really wear togas?
                    -- *Mr. Clueless, San Jose State University*

ANSWER:
Great! Another dumbass who believed his parents and teachers when they said there's no such thing as a stupid question. We have received thousands of e-mails over the years that indisputably prove that your parents and teachers were lying to you. Not only are there stupid questions, but there are many stupid people as well.

[Editors' Note: By printing this question and our corresponding (patronizing) response, we in no way mean to imply that everyone at San Jose State University is as clueless as the guy who sent us this question.]

Alright, Mr. Clueless, do you know what a "Keg Party" is? If you answered "a party where beer is served out of a keg," give yourself one (1) point. Do you know what a "Birthday Party" is? If you answered "a party that celebrates someone's birthday," give yourself two (2) points. And if you're actually keeping score, subtract three (3) points and then slap yourself across the face for being such a moron.

Ok, back to the original question about toga parties. Yes, people really do wear togas to a toga party. If they didn't wear togas, do you know what it would be called instead of "a toga party"? That's right, it would just be called "a party." Ever been to one of those? [probably not] Anyway, you don't need to go out and buy anything special for a toga party; if you have a bed sheet, you have a toga. Simply wrap a sheet around your body, over one shoulder or two (depending on how sexy you're feeling), and then fasten it together with safety pins, knots, duct tape, staples, Velcro, 3 packs of recently chewed watermelon flavored bubblegum, or whatever else your creative mind comes up with. [Ok, sorry, we know you're not very smart, so stick with the safety pins.]

One last piece of advice would be to make sure that the party really is a toga party before you show up in your toga. Because you're probably the kind of dumbass who could easily be duped into wearing a toga to a regular, everyday party - and that might just result in embarrassment of "need-to-transfer" proportions!

-- The College Guy

P.S. In regard to your bed sheet selection, history has shown that light colors (white, yellow, pink, etc.) tend to make the best togas. Those Mickey Mouse & Donald Duck sheets that you've had since you were 6? You'll probably want to leave those at home. And if you're sexually active (or a guy whose only release comes in the form of wet dreams), you'll definitely want to examine your toga sheet carefully for potentially humiliating stains.

QUESTION:
I know I need to break-up with my boyfriend, but I just haven't gotten around to it yet. I really don't want to hurt him. So what's a good time to do it?
   -- Putting Off the Inevitable, University of Michigan

ANSWER:
That's really sweet that you don't want to hurt him (cough, cough), but unless he didn't care about you in the first place (or if he's banging your roommate on the side) then chances are pretty good that you're going to end up hurting him anyway. That's just the way it goes. Break-ups suck.

Anyway, getting back to your question... Sorry, but unfortunately there really is no "*good*" time to break-up with someone. If he's going to be hurt by it, he's going to be hurt by it no matter how or when you do it. The only thing you can do (both to make it easier on him and to keep yourself from being inducted in the Bitch-Of-All-Bitches Hall of Shame) is make sure you don't dump him on any of the following "Break-up Black Out Dates":

- ✓ At a funeral
- ✓ At a wedding
- ✓ Valentine's Day (or three days on either side)
- ✓ His Birthday (or three days on either side)
- ✓ Super Bowl Sunday
- ✓ The day his father goes in for open-heart surgery
- ✓ The week that anyone in his family gets diagnosed with cancer

Other than those occasions, one day is pretty much the same as any other, so just do it as tactfully as possible. [Note to Guys: Those same Break-up Black Out Dates apply to guys too, unless you want to be in the "Dick-Of-All-Dicks Hall of Shame".]

-- The College Guy

QUESTION:
Even though I think I know the answer to this question... which would be that I'm just a stupid girl, I am going to ask you anyway. So here goes nothing. I'm in a long distance relationship (exactly 200 miles apart). I love him so much! He has made me so happy, it is unbelievable. Then last November he "almost" cheated on me. I broke up with him but within the next 10 days we were back together. Then in February I guess he was hooking up with some girl. So we broke up yet again. But I still talk to him everyday. Every conversation we fight, and he tells me how much he loves me blah blah blah, and I believe him. But I know he will just do it again right? Is it possible that he does love me and he is just retarded? How can he do that to me if he really does love me?

-- Naive Girl, Boston College

ANSWER:
Ever hear a saying about "having your cake and eating it too?" Well, your boyfriend is doing just that. You are the "cake," the girl he "loves" and has a history with (which he might not be ready to let go of, and he probably doesn't even realize that he's not ready to let go of it/you -- this is extremely typical of college-aged guys). And the "eating it too" part would be any other girl who causes a twitch in his pants and with whom he thinks he's got any shot of hooking up.

Obviously the 200-mile distance is too great and/or the frequency with which one of you makes the 200-mile booty call is not great enough for this guy if he's letting his one-eyed monster out of its cage every time he thinks he can get some ass.

Two hundred miles isn't exactly continents away. Yes, it can seem far, especially if you don't have easy-access transportation, but it's not like it's an overseas relationship. If your relationship is supposed to be anything close to monogamous, then he's completely disrespecting you and your so-called relationship every time his boxer-briefs go from waist to ankles for any other girl (we're giving him the benefit of the doubt that he's not a tighty-whities guy).

We can't tell you if he loves you, but chances are he's not viewing you as "the love of his life" if he's working his mojo with other chicks. You want to know "how can he do that" to you if he really loves you? It's probably a combination of the fact that he's extremely horny and (you might want to sit down for this one), his feelings for you might not be quite as strong as your feelings for him. You say that he has made you "unbelievably happy" but you're obviously not unbelievably happy right now if you've resorted to asking us for advice.

If you think that he's suddenly going to realize the error of his ways and transform into the faithful Prince Charming you're hoping for, well, you're living in a fantasy land of denial. Rise above it. Don't be *that girl*! Lay down the law and take a stand against this cheating hornball. Either he's going to be faithful, or you're finding yourself another guy - and that should be the bottom line. Third, fourth, and twelfth chances make you into *that girl* and it means that he's walking all over you because you're letting him have his cake and eat it too.

-The College Guy

QUESTION:

Is it ok to transfer to another institution because of financial reasons?

-- Money Problems, Centenary College

ANSWER:

If by "financial reasons" you mean an inability to pay tuition or living expenses, then YES, TRANSFERRING FOR FINANCIAL REASONS IS OK.

But, if by "financial reasons" you mean an inability to sufficiently fund your intravenous drug addiction, habitual gambling problem, or daily visits to strip clubs and happy-ending massage parlors, well, then NO, TRANSFERRING FOR FINANCIAL REASONS IS NOT OK.

-- The College Guy

QUESTION:

I don't really go out to clubs, bars, or parties. So, what are some of the other places where I will be able to meet some good-looking girls?

-- Not a big party guy, Georgia Tech

ANSWER:

Of course you don't go to clubs, bars, or parties – you go to Georgia Institute of Technology! (which, by the way, is about 99.7% male!)

Anyway, if you're not into the party scene, our guess is you want a girl who is intelligent, somewhat conservative, and cares about things besides getting hammered and dancing on bars. But you also want her to be attractive (which is understandable), so here's one secret hiding place for the girls you seek: the library. And since we happen to know that Georgia Tech, ironically enough, has a popular bar near campus called The Library, we'll specify the real, non-alcohol-serving library.

Ironically enough, some of the most social places on campus are college libraries. And the good news is that you will likely be meeting people who also care about doing well in school, graduating, and either continuing studies after college or having a career (there are other places we could direct you if you're just looking to scoop up a brainless ditz with no ambition, but we'll save that for a future column).

The other good news is that there are actually a lot of girls who want to meet guys like you - guys who are intelligent, ambitious, good-looking (you *are* good-looking, right?), and who aren't necessarily wrapped up in the whole party scene. The only bad news, which hopefully you can deal with, is that if you don't go to clubs, bars, or parties, you are not going to meet girls who are dressed to be at clubs, bars, or parties. Sure, they may be pretty. But you'd better be cool with girls in baggy sweatpants, 'cause that might be what you get at the library.

Bonus Answer *(to unasked question)*
The more difficult question to answer is not "where" to meet people, but "how" to meet people. Because, as sad a societal statement as this may be, it can not be argued that it is exponentially easier to meet people when alcohol is involved.

Throughout history, the best way to meet people (other than becoming a contestant on a Reality TV Show) has been through friends of friends - assuming you actually do have a friend or two. So you've got to find a way to put yourself in social settings with some of your friends and everyone should be helping everyone else out by bringing a friend or two from a different social circle. [Example: When you're hanging out with friends from your dorm, invite a few friends from one of your classes. And have some of your friends from your class bring some friends from *their* dorm. Friends-of-friends networking is a simple way to meet new people and expand your circle of acquaintances.]

Maybe you'll all get tickets for a sporting event or a concert. Maybe you'll get a group together either to cook or go out for dinner. Maybe you'll invite everybody over to watch the Sopranos on Sundays, The Apprentice on Thursdays, or Monday Night Football on – surprise, surprise – Mondays. It doesn't matter what the actual activity is, it just takes a little planning and a few friends to each invite a few other friends and before you know it, you'll be meeting tons of new people, and eventually you'll be meeting new people who are friends with the new people you just met -- kinda like a chain of those annoying-ass email forwards, only not as annoying.

-- The College Guy

QUESTION
How do I get a hot girl? I mean a really, REALLY hot girl.
-- Hat, Bloomsburg University

ANSWER:
It is often said that "you can't please everyone," but we're sure gonna try. Much like those choose-your-own-adventure books (the ones we all cheated on as kids by flipping to the back), we invite you to peruse the two responses below and choose whichever one you most agree with. [*Hint:* Girls, choose #1. Guys, choose #2.]

CHOICE #1:
Stop being such a jerk who only cares about how hot a girl is. Doesn't personality mean anything? You're a pig.

CHOICE #2:
Ok, let's cut through all the overly-analytical and philosophical dialogue on what constitutes beauty and how important looks really are.... We all know the type of girl you're talking about.

You're talking about the kind of girl that could make a guy cut off his thumb, pass up Super Bowl tickets, and watch a 48-hour Trading Spaces marathon just for a chance! Yes sir, we're talking about the kind of girl who, when seen in public with you, makes you the automatic envy of every guy that walks by. Yes sir we're talking about the kind of girl so hot that the entire Dallas Cowboys' Cheerleading Squad could walk by and your head wouldn't turn an inch.

So how do you get one of these ridicu-hotties? Well, generally all it takes to attract such a goddess is to be a movie star, rock star, or a multi-millionaire with a 12-inch... um... wallet. Hmmm, doesn't sound like you? Well don't you worry. AskTheCollegeGuy.com has you covered with three can't-miss, surefire strategies for getting that girl you've got no business being with (or at least to get slapped by her).

Switching Teams: This strategy is complicated; but if pulled off properly, it results in both getting the girl and the greatest story you'll ever be able to tell without talking out of your exit-only end. All you need to do is pick the hottie of your dreams and let her overhear you saying three magic words: *I am gay.*

The next thing you know you will be "one of the girls," granted access a straight man could never dream of (especially if that straight man is you). After a few months of facials, long cries into the night, several pints of Ben

& Jerry's, and a steady dialogue about what pigs men are, you and your hottie will be as inseparable as... well... as inseparable as a hottie and her best gay friend can be.

Soon she'll start saying things like "if only you weren't gay..." or "why can't I find a straight guy as perfect as you?" Then, when you feel the time is right, you have *The Talk*. You're very confused, meeting her has caused all sorts of feelings you didn't know you could have, you don't know what to do, this is all so frightening but at the same time kind of exciting, etc etc. Pow! You've gone from favorite safe-friend to man of her dreams in no time and she'll be dying to help you explore your new feelings.

Right Time, Right Place: Picture this scenario: The quarterback for your school's football team and his insanely hot girlfriend are at the same party as you -- how you got invited is still a mystery, but that's not the point. [*Editors' note: If your school doesn't have football, you may substitute "captain of the debate team" or "secretary of the chemistry club" - we hear they pull the hotties at some schools.*] Anyway, half a keg into the night and our pretty princess notices her jackass of a boyfriend is getting a little too flirty with the head cheerleader. Next thing you know, they're fighting and she declares it over. As she stomps away, our jilted gem is going to be looking for some guy, any guy, to make her former flame as jealous as possible. Strategically place yourself in the right place at the right time as she prepares to make her exit, and you could be the lucky fellow she chooses as her instrument of revenge. Next thing you know, you'll be living the fantasy you could only... well... imagine.

Sure, it won't last long and she's bound to return to the old boyfriend and send you packing in a matter of days - if not hours. But takes a few pictures (or conveniently place a web-cam) and the memories will last even longer than the black eyes the boyfriend is likely to give you when he finds out what you did.

Honesty: If none of the above works, you'll have to acknowledge that the only fool-proof way to "get a hot girl" is complete and utter honesty. Here's what we mean: Perfect an authentic-sounding accent, and then tell the object of your lust that your name is Prince Humperdink from the Island of Krypton Falls, located in the Voldemort Sea right between Naboo and Fraggle Rock. You are the only son of King Anheuiser Starbuck, therefore making you heir to the throne of Dakota and on your 25th birthday you stand to inherit $75 million in rare baseball cards. Sure your entire relationship will be based on a series of randomly concocted lies that really make no sense at all, but if you say it all with confidence, it should work. Besides, look where honesty has gotten you so far -- you're pinning your relationship hopes on the guidance of an overly-sarcastic, entertain-the-masses, talking-out-of-ass, advice columnist who sleeps until noon, consistently writes with a hangover, and has been trying to get this damn book published for the last 3 years!

Good luck.

-- The College Guy

QUESTION:
This guy on my hall is in one of my classes and always comes to me to copy my homework. I don't want to say no, but I am sick of doing all the work. So what should I do?
-- Help Me Make it Stop,
Washington University in St. Louis

ANSWER:

A great 13th century philosopher once said: "Allow yourself to be used, and you will soon be abused." We find these words to be quite appropriate to your situation. [*Note from the College Guy: We're almost certain that was the same philosopher that said: "Go to bed with itchy bum, wake up with smelly finger."*]

OK, so that's not really a quote from a great philosopher. Heck, it's not even a quote from a bad fortune cookie. But seriously, don't let yourself get walked all over like George McFly (Marty's dad in Back To The Future). If you're sick of doing this guy's work for him, tell him exactly that. We realize that could be easier said than done if this guy is older than you, bigger than you, more popular than you, or all of the above. But unless you're content to keep doing this guy's homework for him, you've just got to suck it up and tell your Biff Tannon the arrangement is over. [*Note: In a perfect world, you could tell him that you don't feel right about violating the Honor Code. But we here at AskTheCollegeGuy. com our realists, and as unfortunate as this may be, that response would probably get laughed at by the majority of college students - particularly the ones that would ask you to do their homework for them in the first place*]

Regardless of how you tell this guy that your days of doing his work are over, be prepared to fall quickly out of favor with him and his friends. But if he was just using you to do his homework for him in the first place, chances are he's not the best guy for you to be hanging out with anyway - and he's certainly not someone you'd want to call a real friend.

The bigger question here might be "How and why did you get yourself in this situation in the first place?" Our guess is that you were just trying to be nice and to help the guy out at first. And saying "No" can be pretty difficult when you're struggling to fit in and gain acceptance -- but trust us on this one, you're not gaining anybody's acceptance if all you are is the smart kid they can get to do their homework. You're trying to fit in with the wrong crowd if you have to do unreciprocated favors to make them like you. Good luck McFly.

-- The College Guy

QUESTION:
Does a college student's GPA go down because they are in a long distance relationship with someone?

-- George, Wake Forest

ANSWER:
For starters, if you're looking for a "yes" answer just so you'll have a valid reason to get out of your current long distance relationship then you really shouldn't be in the relationship in the first place.

There are obviously a lot of things that will contribute to how you do in the classroom, the most obvious of which is how much you actually go to class, how much you study, and how good you are at bullshitting your way through tests, papers, and in-class discussion (it also helps to be able to concentrate with a hangover).

The reason that a long-distance relationship, a varsity sport, pledging a fraternity/sorority, or any number of other activities is believed to have a negative effect on your GPA doesn't have nearly as much to do with the actual activity as it does with how much time you devote to the activity (or more specifically, how much time your relationship or other activity takes away from your academics).

There are only 24 hours in a day (unless you live in Montana, Nebraska, Idaho, Mississippi, or New Jersey) so you have to figure out how much time you need to devote to your academics to maintain whatever grade level you - or your parents - want you to maintain.

If your long-distance relationship (weekend visits, talking on the phone with him/her, e-mailing, instant-messaging, trying to come up with stories to cover up the fact that you cheated on him/her with somebody you met while drunk at a party ... um, ok, sorry, scratch that last one)... anyway, if all the aspects of your long-distance relationship interfere with going to class, studying, and devoting the necessary time to your academics, then yes, the long-distance relationship will indirectly contribute to a lower GPA. But it's really how you manage your time more than the actual relationship (so don't use your long-distance relationship as a scapegoat excuse for why you're failing Bio or Econ).

                                                    -- The College Guy

Chapter Five
-JANUARY-

QUESTION:

I was at a party with friends on New Year's Eve. Everybody was drinking and then at midnight everybody was giving everybody little New Year's kisses. But the kiss I got from my friend Christine was much more than a little New Year's peck! It was open mouth, and.... tongue!!!! In case you can't tell from how freaked out I am, she's a girl and I'm a girl and we're both straight (at least I thought we both were). Does this mean she's a lesbian? And what should I say the next time I see her?

-- In Shock, Rochester

ANSWER:

No, it doesn't mean she's a lesbian... it means *you're* a lesbian! Yep, that's right, no more dick for you, you're officially a full-fledged homosexual woman now so you'd better start embracing it.

Ok, sorry, just kidding. But seriously, you need to relax! This is only a big deal if you choose to make it a big deal. While it might be a new and shocking experience for you, this is far from the first time a college girl has ever kissed (or been kissed by) another girl. And no, it doesn't necessarily mean that your friend is a lesbian. This little alcohol-induced, lip-locking, tongue-twirling, ass-grabbing, breast-fondling, New Year's Eve experience doesn't say anything one way or the other about your sexuality or hers.

[Editors' Note: We know you didn't mention any ass-grabbing or breast-fondling; we just added that part for our enjoyment and the enjoyment of our readers.]

So why did she kiss you? Maybe she was so drunk she didn't know what she was doing. Maybe it's something she's always been curious about and the alcohol coupled with the New Year's festivities just lowered her inhibitions about it. Maybe you're just so damn sexy that neither gender can resist you. Maybe Ashton Kutcher was abducted by aliens, temporarily inserted into your friend's body, and you were actually being Punk'd!

There could be any number of reasons why you and your friend ended up making out. (And we hope you can appreciate that we haven't even suggested the possibility that *you* might have knowingly or unknowingly actually encouraged your friend's behavior... nor have we asked if a small part of you secretly enjoyed the whole thing; after all, once you realized it was open mouth, was there really no time for you to pull away before tongues got involved?) Anyway, we'll continue and assume that it was a complete shock to you and that you did not enjoy it.

So how do you handle the situation now? We would suggest you initially just act as though nothing out of the ordinary happened, don't let it bother you, and wait to see if your friend approaches you about it. Now that she's sobered up, your friend may be really embarrassed about it and she'll want to talk to you about it to make sure everything is still cool between you two (either that or she'll be so uncomfortable and humiliated that she'll immediately start looking at transfer applications).

Regardless of whether you or she initiates the conversation, you definitely need to at least mention it (not because it is necessarily that big a deal, but just because it's clearly bothering you and it doesn't seem like you'll just be able to forget about it). So if she doesn't come to you about it, you need to somehow casually bring it up yourself. But don't do it in front of other people, don't try to make a big deal about it, and don't try to make her feel stupid or embarrass her. And if you get the sense that she might actually be having issues or questioning her sexuality, tread carefully and don't try to pull her out of that proverbial closet if that's where it seems she'd prefer to stay (that's not your decision to make for her).

But the bottom line for you is that you should stop freaking out and realize it's not a big deal. If you were Britney and she was Madonna and the kiss took place in front of millions of people at the 2003 MTV Video Music Awards, ***then*** it would be a big deal. But as far as your situation goes, only three things have changed as far as you should be concerned:

1. You now have something else to admit to the next time you're playing "Truth or Dare" or "I Never..."
2. You just became a heck of a lot more intriguing in the eyes of any guy who finds out about this (since the idea of one day possibly getting you and your friend into a threesome will make the average guy go nuts)
3. You are now a lesbian.

-- ***The College Guy***

QUESTION:

I've been hanging out with this girl for a couple months. We've never had "*the talk*" so I don't know if she's really my girlfriend, but I heard she slept with 3 different guys over Christmas Break. Some of my friends say I have a right to be pissed and some say it's not a big deal since she's not really my girlfriend. What do you think?

-- *James, Colgate*

ANSWER:

We think you're dating a slut! ... But more importantly, what do you think? Talk to her and see what she has to say (both about her promiscuity over break and about where things stand between the two of you). We know it can suck to have "the talk," but if you don't even know whether or not to be mad because she's sleeping around, then clearly you need to figure some things out. And that probably means having at least "a talk" if not "the talk" with your kinda-sorta-girlfriend-chick.

-- *The College Guy*

QUESTION:

Hey, I was just wondering on how to get rid of a hangover before a test?

-- *Jessica, UCLA*

ANSWER:

In case any parents are reading this answer: **Shame on you! You shouldn't be getting hammered the night before a test.**

[Parents, please close the book now]

Now, if you *do* happen to drink the night before a test (or any night for that matter), be sure to drink a glass of water as soon as you get home and walk in the door. Drink another glass of water before you take off your party clothes and change into whatever sexy threads you sleep in. Drink another glass of water after you've changed clothes (possibly while you're drunk-dialing, drunk-texting, drunk-emailing, or whatever other post-drinking habit you may have). If you actually remember to drink all that water, you'll probably have to take a leak by now (if so, drink one more glass of water while you're in the bathroom - either before, after, or during urination). Fill that glass up one more time before you crawl into bed and set it by your bed (but not too close that you'll knock it over if you start thrashing around in your sleep, dreaming about the hottie you wish you'd brought home with you).

That won't necessarily stop Hurricane Hangover from coming ashore, but it should at least downgrade the hangover to Tropical Storm level.

A better question is not how to get rid of a hangover before a test, but how to get rid of a test during a hangover. Too bad you didn't ask ***that*** question!

-- The College Guy

P.S. If you do happen to skip the class and miss the test, whatever excuse you come up with, do NOT say it was because your grandmother died. For starters, that's the second most common excuse professors will hear (right behind the always vague "I was sick"). But more importantly, if your grandmother is still alive, using her death as an excuse might *actually* kill her. It's true! It is well-documented that many college students have inadvertently killed many grandparents via the bad karma that enters the universe when false grandparent death claims are given as an excuse to miss class. [We got an e-mail forward about that once, so it must be true] Plus, when your grandmother does actually croak, it'll be a real tragedy -- because you'll need to think up another excuse for missing class!

-- *The College Guy*

QUESTION:
Hey, I am sick and tired of liking guys and them not returning the favor. The only thing that I wish I had more of would be boobs. Do you think that is my problem?

-- *Sophomore Needing Attention, Louisville*

ANSWER:
OK, we're going to fight back the urge to fire away with the first sarcastic response that comes to mind after reading your question. So this is going to be another rare question where AskTheCollegeGuy.com is going to be completely serious for a minute because we have a very specific, well thought-out theory about breasts that we need to share.

Think of every girl you know. Got it? Okay, now picture all their breasts. *[Editors' Note: Yes, that's a whole lot of boobs! If you're a guy reading this, pick yourself up off the floor and/ or put away the tissue box. If you're a girl reading this, please just continue reading and ignore this note.]* Anyway, now that you're picturing the breasts of every girl you know, we want you to think about how each girl likely feels about her own breasts. Don't most of them complain about one thing or another?

The girls who have small breasts are usually jealous of their more well-endowed friends. These small-breasted girls wear bras designed to increase cleavage and/or make their boobs appear bigger and some might even talk about someday getting implants.

Many girls who have big breasts often complain they're too big, are bothered by guys always staring at their chests, have trouble finding comfortable sports bras for jogging, and some might end up needing breast reduction later in life for medical reasons.

Very, very, very, very few women are completely content with the rack they were dealt via their natural genetic makeup. Chances are you're always going to want to add a little or subtract a little – even if you're blessed with a nice perky pair of B's or C's that the girls with A's and DD's would kill for.

And while there are obviously plenty of guys out there who like big breasts, the fact is that there are also plenty of guys out there who like smaller breasts. *[Editors' Note: No, we're not just saying that to make you feel better about your smaller breasts - if you've ever read our column before, you know we really don't care if our answers make you feel better or not.]*

Just because loud, boisterous, macho-guy locker-room talk is more likely to include "Did you see the huge tits on that girl?" rather than "Did you see the firm, small to average-sized tits that are perfectly proportional to the rest of the body on that girl?" does NOT mean that the former is always preferred to the latter -- it just may tend to be more worthy of or conducive to a public comment.

In conclusion, there's no question that the average (heterosexual) guy loves having his hands on a woman's breasts (perhaps even more than having the remote-control in one hand and a beer in the other), but as enjoyable as a great rack can be, the size of your breasts will rarely make or break a relationship – or even a random hookup – even with the most superficially shallow of guys.

So unfortunately for the Louisville sophomore who sent in this question, if you're not getting the guys you want, it's not because of your small boobs. So you've probably got other issues you don't even know about! Good luck figuring out what those might be.

-- The College Guy

QUESTION:
I think it sucks that all the hot girls always go for the asshole guys. Why do nice guys always finish last?

-- Nice Guy in Last Place, Stanford

ANSWER:
First, we have to point out that not "all" girls go for asshole guys (some, of course, are lesbians and prefer girls). But since it does seem to happen more often than it should (particularly since it happens *in spite of* most girls who claim that all they want is "a nice guy"), we'll go ahead and give you AskTheCollegeGuy.com's take on "The Asshole-Guy Phenomenon."

Let's take a look at the assholes you're talking about. *[Desperately fighting off a proctologist joke]* Many of them are cocky, arrogant, and don't have much respect for other people, right? We don't want to oversimplify this because we all know there can be many different types of assholes, but in most cases these guys act this way for one reason: because they can.

They know they can get away with acting pretty much any way they want without suffering too many negative consequences, primarily because they have other qualities or characteristics which have always offset their asshole behaviors. Let's examine the common themes.

✓ Many of the assholes on your campus may come from a wealthy family. Money contributes to a big ego (a common asshole-characteristic) because they are accustomed to always having whatever they want, whenever they want it, so they feel they don't need to be nice to people.

✓ Many of the assholes on your campus are good-looking guys. For better or worse, the reality of our society is that most people are attracted, at least first and foremost, to physical (external) beauty. So, the good-looking guys are accustomed to being able to attract the good-looking girls with minimal effort.

✓ Many of the assholes on your campus are in a fraternity or play a varsity sport. Athletes and frat guys don't have to worry about being nice in order to gain acceptance by others, establish their own identity, or make new friends since all that generally comes right along with being on the team or in the fraternity.

Important Note: Please don't take this to mean that anybody with any of the above-mentioned characteristics is automatically an asshole. Obviously there are some people who have some or all of the above going for them and still manage to be nice guys too. Of course, those are the guys that usually end up with Jennifer Aniston, Sarah Michelle Gellar, and Janet Jackson. And one note to all the self-proclaimed "nice guys" out there: You end up being somewhat of an asshole yourself if you pre-judge someone else to be an asshole just because they can get a girl that you can't. We've heard Brad Pitt, Freddy Prinze Jr., and Jermaine Dupree are all pretty cool guys.

Anyway, now that we have an idea of what the asshole is all about, let's take a quick look at why so many girls go ga-ga over them.

It's really pretty simple. For starters, many girls in college don't know what they're looking for. While they know they'll want a nice guy at some point in the future to settle down with (assuming celebrity bad-boys like Collin Ferrell are unattainable), that future is a long ways off for many college girls and they have no idea what kind of guys they should be looking for now. They'll initially be attracted to the asshole's good looks. Then they will be impressed with the confidence with which the asshole carries himself. *[Note: There's a blurred line between confidence and ego-driven-arrogance.]* Finally, as a varsity athlete or a fraternity guy, it is assumed that the asshole is a popular guy with lots of friends, and therefore he is socially acceptable and someone that her friends will be impressed by. And it's generally not until an argument, fight, or break-up that the girl realizes the guy was an asshole.

-- *The College Guy*

QUESTION:
Hmm.....Where do I start... Well, say you meet this girl and she's super hot... Then you to get to know her and she's pretty cool. You end up sleeping with her a couple of times and there's no damage to the "relationship" you now have with her... but (the big 'but') you soon find out that she's not how old she said she was... but she's really young... like 15 (holy shit)... she admits to it but she still wants to bone, I mean hang out, what the hell can you do to get out of this shit? Oh yeah, she also said that if you "hurt her" or basically break up with the lying bitch, she'll tell her dad. Free ticket to jail! Now what do ya do?

-- *Jake With No Paddle, Up Shit's Creek*

ANSWER:
Our initial reaction: Holy sh*t! You are completely f*cked!

After a second reading, our secondary reaction: Holy sh*t! What a manipulative little bitch! You are completely f*cked!

After a third reading, our final reaction: Holy sh*t! There is almost no way that this ends with a happy ending. You are completely f*cked!

This is one of very few cases in which we really feel that you could be royally screwed no matter what direction you go in. No matter what advice we give, you could theoretically find your ass in jail (with a cellmate named Bubba). You've probably already played these situations out a thousand times in your head... but here is a list of some random ideas that were bounced around the AskTheCollegeGuy.com Board Room during our last staff meeting (for the record, we don't necessarily recommend any of the following, because the way we see it, you're pretty much screwed - no pun intended - either way). But here goes with the random lists of "We don't really recommend it, but...

- ✓ Talk to your parents - you'll need them on your side if this thing turns ugly.
- ✓ Talk to a lawyer - find out everything you can about statutory rape laws in your state.

[Note: Despite the gravity of the situation, hopefully you can at least take a small bit of comfort in the fact that you are living out the fantasy of almost every guy reading this right now - you're literally being forced to have sex with a smokin' hot teen-ager!]

- ✓ From the "could blow up in your face" department - you could call her bluff about "telling daddy" and go talk to her father yourself, explaining how sorry you are and that you would have never done anything like this if you'd known how old she was.

[Note: We figure you've got a 50-50 shot that he already knows his daughter is a manipulative little slut and he won't hold you responsible at all. Of course there's also a chance that his reaction will involve a shotgun and your testicles.]

- ✓ You could flip out and start crying, let her think you've got screwed up emotional issues, so that maybe she'll dump you and set you free from this teen version of Fatal Attraction.
- ✓ You could fake an STD (sexually transmitted disease) and maybe she wouldn't want to touch you anymore.
- ✓ Without sending her running off to cry "statutory rape" to Daddy, any chance you can just slowly get her to lose interest in you? Be very very careful if you try anything like this (or the two above), because you DON'T want to piss her off and set off the ticking time-bomb you've been sleeping with.

If you *do* continue sleeping with her, just remember *that this* is not a girl to trust if she says "don't worry about a condom, I'm on the pill." Additionally, if you *do* continue sleeping with her, bring YOUR OWN condoms. This is the type of girl that wouldn't think twice about poking a hole in the condom and hoping that an unplanned pregnancy will help you two grow closer.

Good luck. Be careful. May the force be with you. And please, let us know how this one turns out for you. We'll be sure to let you know if we get any good reader feedback for you. And if you end up in jail, we'll definitely send you a free copy of this book (whenever we get around to finishing it) for you and Bubba to share.

-- *The College Guy*

[Editors' Note: When we originally published Jake's predicament on our website, it generated more reader response than we've ever had from one single question/answer column. So, we figured we should share a sample of advice from our readers. Bare in mind, this is from our readers, not us!]

READER RESPONSES TO JAKE'S DILEMMA:

My advice for Jake is to enlist the help of his friends. Best case I can think of is for one of his buddies to "take her away" being very careful not to have sex with this girl, of course, and then when she leaves Jake for the buddy, have the buddy dump her. She'll be mad at the buddy, but the buddy is not over a barrel. She won't be mad at Jake and therefore won't get him in trouble. Here's hoping it works!

-- Tyler

Totally turn the tables and start "falling in love" with her. Slowly start getting way too lovey dovey, try to hang out with her 24-7, get jealous over the slightest mention of another guy. It'll be such a turn-off that she'll want nothing to do with you -- and hopefully this girl is as stupid as she is manipulative.

-- Kristen

Here's a way out of that trap. He should go to her father and ask for her hand (and I guess the rest of her) in marriage. Yeah, that's right, put your money where your mouth is... If the father says hell no! At least the relationship is out in the open and the guy can exit gracefully. Chances are the father isn't going to try to jail a guy that wants to marry his daughter. If the father says hell yes! The guy can then get into the whole let's plan a big wedding thingy. He can say "I want to wait at least a year to be able to afford a nice ring." I want to book our wedding on the 18th hole at Pebble Beach (waiting list at least 2 years) - get it? A wedding properly planned can take up to 3 years.

-- Anna

Dude, I don't see the problem... You said she was super hot, right? You said she still wants to bone, right? So where's the problem bro?

-- Mikey

I had an experience just like his. I went out with this guy but it turned out he was 16 (me being 22) wasn't a good idea. Well the way I got out of the whole jail thing is, I told him I was dying. I told him I had a brain tumor from having too much sex (which we all know can't happen) but he believed it. I told him that I needed to find myself before I died. He believed me and I got out of the statutory rape thing.

-- Jessica

Jake, remember she is young and dumb so it's easy to get into her head. No matter how manipulative she is, she is only fifteen. Don't sleep with her again because in court if the D.A. asks you If you slept with her after you found out her age then you are screwed. Don't piss her off but don't sleep with her. Try to be like a big brother to her. Don't break up with her or she'll turn into Alicia Silverstone in "The Crush". Be a friend and if she asks "what's the matter" then tell her you are having problems at school, work and home. Remember the more drama you have in your life the less she wants to be involved. Become boring and blame it on one of the three above. Last but not least, if she keeps pushing the sex issue, then tell her that waiting makes sex more exciting and you want to tease her by making her wait. Eventually she will start hanging out more with her friends and some guy her age will lay it down for her and she will screw him and she will leave you alone. Girls that age seem to change their mind a lot. Good luck.

-- David

Chapter Six
-February-

QUESTION:

My girlfriend is planning to go down to Mardi Gras with her friends. I've never been so I really don't know what it's all about, but my friends say I should be worried about letting her go. Is it really that bad?

-- *Gavin, Oregon State*

ANSWER:

First off, we apologize to all the raging feminists out there who are asking, "What do you mean 'let' her go? She's free to do whatever the hell she wants, you male-chauvinist pig!"). Anyway, before we address the question of whether you should "let" her go, there's something more important for us to do. Since you clearly don't even seem to know what Mardi Gras really is in the first place, we feel obligated to educate you:

What Is Mardi Gras?

Well, the *historical* significance of Mardi Gras has to do with the observance of a "Carnival" before the Lenten period (a Christian symbolic penitence from Ash Wednesday to Easter)...

But let's be honest, that's not exactly the reason so many college students descend upon New Orleans for Mardi Gras every year...

- ✓ Thousands and thousands and thousands of drunk people partying in the streets of New Orleans (actually, we think it's probably over a million, but since we can't verify that, we'll stick with "thousands and thousands and thousands.")
- ✓ Everyone is wearing beads and other decorative necklaces that they somehow "earned" (more on that below).
- ✓ Most commonly heard phrase is "Show Your Tits" (which will frequently be chanted by mobs of drunk and horny guys).
- ✓ Girls lifting their shirts is just one way to "earn" beads at Mardi Gras. People can get very creative with what they ask others to do for beads, but sexually-related requests are most common.
- ✓ Public drunkenness, open container, and indecent exposure (girls lifting shirts and both genders dropping their pants) are among the violations of laws that police will usually ignore in the crowded streets of the French Quarter during Mardi Gras. The main concern of New Orleans police during Mardi Gras is to prevent violence, theft and other more serious crimes which tend to happen at Mardi Gras with the streets packed with people. *NOTE: Plenty of people do still manage to get arrested, so be careful.*
- ✓ Extremely crowded, particularly on and around Bourbon Street, so if you're not holding someone's hand, it is easy to get separated from your friends and end up with a girl named Tammy from SMU who takes you back to her hotel room at 4 in the

morning, takes off all her clothes, and takes off all your clothes, just before her boyfriend (a big dude named Todd) starts banging on the door and you're forced to jump out a window onto the back of a truck and... *[What? No, um, that didn't happen to anyone we know. That was just a hypothetical, honest.]*

✓ With all these partiers in such a compact area, with all the alcohol being consumed, and with these magical colored beads taking on such inflated value in the barter market, New Orleans is inexplicably turned into a Mecca for nudity and sexual promiscuity during Mardi Gras.

Anyway, to get back to the initial question about your girlfriend going to Mardi Gras... we're not going to directly answer that question except to say that it all depends on what she thinks is acceptable behavior while in a relationship, what you think is acceptable behavior while in a relationship, and the level of trust in your particular relationship. You know her better than we do (or so you hope!). But if you think she might get a little crazy down there, feel free to send us a picture of her so we can look for her on the next edition of Girls Gone Wild - College Co-eds at Mardi Gras.

-- The College Guy

QUESTION:
I am transferring to a new school and I am very nervous about making friends and fitting in. I really need advice. I need major help. Also, how do I make sure people like me? This is really important and I'm really nervous about this. Help me! Please!!!

-- Tony, University of Buffalo

ANSWER:
First of all, CHILL OUT! You need to relax and quit freakin' out. You seem way too uptight about this, so we're just

guessing that the reason you transferred in the first place is because things weren't going so well for you socially at your other school? Maybe people didn't like you? So maybe you think you just need a fresh start?

Anyway, the biggest thing we can suggest is to just be yourself, but we should probably expound upon that a little bit. By the way, the original, pre-edited version of your question was written about as well as my 12-year-old cousin used to write... when she was 7! But don't worry, since you don't seem like the brightest bulb on the tree, we'll try to use as many monosyllabic words as possible. [Sorry about that, just kidding, obviously you have no idea what monosyllabic means. It's Portuguese for "short".]

Moving right along.... The phrase "be yourself" has been around so long that many people have forgotten its meaning. That's partly because people don't really understand themselves and who they really are. And it's definitely a good idea to have a clear understanding of yourself before you can expect anyone else to understand you (or like you). Ask yourself a bunch of questions: "What do I like to do? What makes me genuinely happy? What kind of people do I like being around? What do I want people to think of when they hear my name? What are some of my better qualities? Do I like prefer gay porn or movies about gladiators?"

You want people to be attracted to the real you and not just some image you're trying to portray. Example: You can't dress and act like Eminem with the hopes of people liking you just because lots of people like him. Only he has lived his life, so he's the only one that gets to be Slim Shady. But don't worry, just be yourself and everything will be fine... since you are the only one who has lived *your* life, there's no one out there more qualified than you to be you. *[Editors'*

Note: We're pretty sure we saw that exact line in the closing scene of some cheesy after-school special several years ago. It was likely followed by a parent and child from a dysfunctional family hugging one another in a long embrace before turning and walking back into the house with their arms around one another as music faded in, the closing credits began to roll, and once again some incredibly tragic or complex situation was completely resolved in exactly 60 minutes. Gotta love the after-school-special phenomenon... Timmy gets caught skipping school, gets kicked off the football team, knocks up his girlfriend, gets in a fight with his best friend, smashes his car into a tree while driving drunk, and somehow his entire life gets turned around in 60 minutes and everyone lives happily ever after.]

Wow, talk about getting off topic! Anyway, don't try too hard to get people to like you, take a step back every so often and think about how you come off to other people. Try to slightly modify any behaviors that people might find annoying or offensive. Don't try too hard to impress anybody. And maybe join an activity or two to help you meet some new people. You should start making friends in no time. But if you're still finding yourself in a sad state of affairs and you're not making any friends, you might want to see a professional counselor who might recommend some type of group therapy or adult social skills classes for you. Good luck!

[Editors' Note: Please notice that we consciously refrained from making any jokes throughout the entire last paragraph to show all you readers out there that AskTheCollegeGuy.com is more than just a sarcastic, humor column. We can also be a serious, compassionate, no-nonsense advice column when the situation calls for it.... Oh, screw it, who are we kidding? That guy's not gonna make any more friends at his new school than he had at his old school and he'll fit in about as well as my grandmother fits in at an Usher concert.]

-- The College Guy

QUESTION:
I'm doing a thesis on "Mardi Gras as a license to loose your inhibitions & feed the flesh." I've NEVER done this before, so how do I approach it? Everything I've looked up is more or less how to enjoy Mardi Gras or the history of it. I want to show that it's not so much a religious event (as you think of Easter or Christmas) but more pagan, Sodom & Gomorra type. It's more for the flesh than for the soul. Where do I start?

-- Writing my first research paper,
Forsyth Tech Community College

ANSWER:
First of all, we just answered a Mardi Gras question. Second of all, your question was a little too, um, weird! So we're only giving you three words: Girls Gone Wild.

[Editors' Note: If that answer was too short for you and you would prefer we expound upon that answer with a more detailed response, we'd be happy to. You may find a better understanding of Mardi Gras by viewing any of the following on video or DVD:

Girls Gone Wild II
Girls Gone Wild III
Girls Gone Wild Deluxe Edition
Girls Gone Wild: The Best of Mardi Gras
Girls Gone Wild: Mardi Gras 2K1
Girls Gone Wild: Mardi Gras Co-eds
In Development: Girls Gone Wild, AskTheCollegeGuy.com-style
-- The College Guy

QUESTION:
I'm having an argument with a couple of friends. One thinks that whenever you are driving between cities, you drive "up" from one to the other. The other thinks that driving "up" or

"down" is determined by elevation of the cities. I feel that it should be determined by latitude, north being "up". What's your opinion?

-- Driving Me Bananas, University of Alberta

ANSWER:
We like this question for multiple reasons… not the least of which is that it inflates our already-skewed sense of universal importance when AskTheCollegeGuy.com is called upon to serve as the ultimate authority on ANYTHING!

But before we settle this argument for you and your friends, allow us to take a stroll down Memory Road. [*Editors' Note: Yes, we realize that the more common expression is "Memory Lane" but we prefer "Memory Road" both for the simple sake of being different AND because the word "Road" reminds of the scene in Black Sheep when Chris Farley and David Spade can't pronounce it correctly: Roooooo-adds.*] Ok, never mind… anyway, the two random debates that we have been e-mailed about most frequently over the last few years are:

✓ Britney or Christina
[*Editors' Note #1: This one was a no-brainer in our opinion because Britney's Pepsi commercials were single-handedly the reason we switched from Coke to Pepsi at AskTheCollegeGuy. com headquarters.*]
[*Editors' Note #2: If a Coca-Cola Executive is reading this and would like to offer us money to erase Editors' Note #1, we would pledge our full support to Christina and Coke. No question, we can definitely be bought. Of course, we're so desperate for cash here at AskTheCollegeGuy.com headquarters, we'd probably sell-out at the right price and pledge our eternal endorsement to Tab, RC Cola, or even that generic brand our grandmothers buy at the local grocery store.*]

✓ Smoking "up" vs. Smoking "out"

[Editors' Note: This debate has been waged on college campuses for years! The debate over which preposition in the English language officially makes "smoking" an illegal activity. As you are probably aware, the verb "smoking" can generally refer to tobacco products when used alone. The terms "smoking up" and "smoking out", on the other hand, almost always refers to marijuana/pot/weed/etc. Unfortunately, neither term is officially more acceptable than the others as it is generally a matter of geography that determines which term is officially more acceptable; a gross over-generalization would be that the NorthEast "smokes up" while the West Coast and much of the South "smokes out". Ricky Williams does both.]

For the record, our lawyers have asked us to mention that AskTheCollegeGuy.com does not encourage or condone any illegal drug use… except maybe Nyquil or Tylenol PM.

OK, getting back to the original question from Banana-chick in Alberta... Our official AskTheCollegeGuy.com position is that your first friend is a dumbass (you can NOT drive "up" to Florida from New York). Your second friend is dumb, but not as dumb as your first friend. Even if Denver sits at a higher elevation than many parts of Canada, you would never drive "up" from Canada to Denver. So in conclusion, we officially declare you the victor in this all-important debate you've been having with your friends. Since the invention of maps (and the newer invention of mapquest.com), it is universally accepted that you drive "up" to more northern cities and you drive "down" to more southern cities.

There are, however, a few exceptions to this rule where geographic latitude can be over-ruled. Two such exceptions are the North Pole and the South Pole. Of course, if you ever find yourself in a car at the North or South Pole, you've got much bigger problems than which preposition you should be using to describe your destination.

-- The College Guy

QUESTION:
The other day I saw what looked like a zit on my foreskin. I popped it, not thinking anything about it. Then I thought it could be warts. I'm going to get a physical next month, at which time I'll ask the doctor about it. Should I be really worried about it? I'm kinda freaking out about it. Let me know what you think.

-- J., University of Wisconsin

ANSWER:
Dude!!! We're not gonna touch this one except to say that we think you should get your ass (and your ding-a-ling) into the doctor's office immediately! If you wait for next month, it might fall off!

QUESTION:
College Guy,
I recently was blown off by my boyfriend of 7 months. He wanted to go to a party and I didn't. He went anyway and I was so aggravated that I called my ex to talk. Me and my ex went and got coffee and talked. That was the extent of it. When my boyfriend questioned me about it, I lied. A few days ago I admitted the lie and he broke up with me. I didn't mean to lie, I only didn't want to upset him. I love this guy more than anything in the world. Please help, I'm miserable without him.

-- Miserable, Mount Watchusett Community College

ANSWER:
First of all, why didn't you want to go to the party with him? Are you a social misfit? Does too much fun give you a migraine? Was it that time of the month for you? Or did you have to stay home to watch Sex In The City or a Trading Spaces marathon?

Second, why did you feel the need to lie if all you did was have coffee with the ex-boyfriend? We're guessing it's either one of two things:
1) You've still got some unresolved feelings for your ex-guy and that's why it was a big deal that you were seeing him.
2) This latest boyfriend is too controlling, overly-possessive, and doesn't trust you to be out of his sight so that's why you were scared of him finding out. *[NOTE: We sincerely doubt this is the case or he wouldn't have gone to that party without you in the first place]*

And finally, it is definitely NOT a good sign if your first reaction the minute your boyfriend "aggravates" you, is to call your ex-boyfriend! What does that say about you? You were pissed off at your boyfriend for going to the party without you and you were either looking for some attention or trying to get back at him for neglecting you. Either way, not the most mature reaction on your part.

On the other hand, if conversation was really the only thing exchanged between you and your ex, then you really didn't do anything wrong - well, other than lying about it. But that's all in the past now, so here's how you get him back...

Assuming hypnosis is out of the question, you're going to try an ancient ritual called "Honesty". This is probably a foreign concept to a girl whose first impulse is lie about something as (supposedly) innocent as having coffee, but sit down with him and tell him how hurt you were when he wanted to go to the party and not hang out with you. Explain that you only called your ex- because you were feeling neglected, angry, hurt, and confused, and all you wanted was a little bit of attention, and you only lied about it because you were afraid of losing him over it. Remind him that there was absolutely no physical contact, and tell him why you still want to be with him.

-- ***The College Guy***

P.S. If all that overly-sensitive, pour-your-heart-out, honesty crap doesn't work to get him back, then forget about him and find a new guy. And hopefully you can find a guy who doesn't like parties and hates having fun as much as you do because we still can't figure out why you didn't just go to the damn party with him in the first place!

QUESTION:
Why do some college professors teach an entirely different course than what's on the syllabus?

-- ***Annoyed by Profs, Morehouse College***

ANSWER:
We've heard this question more than once.

Sometimes it is a simple case of a tenured professor arrogantly thinking they know more than the department head, submitting one curriculum to the department head for approval, and continuing to teach whatever the hell they want to.

But sometimes it's much, much worse.... And your problem could be a lot more serious than you realize.

First and foremost, you need to check your syllabus for the time, day, and professor of your class. If any of the three do not match the time, day, and professor on your schedule, then you are a dip-shit. In this case, you have been attending the wrong class all semester and you desperately need to start making an appearance in the class you're likely failing because you've been absent all semester. Once you realize just how bad you are failing and that you will never be able to catch up and receive a passing grade, you need to beg, plead, or blackmail a Dean to let you drop the class and take it another semester.

-- *The College Guy*

QUESTION:
My Roommate is homosexual. I'm not gay, and I don't have anything against anyone that is, but I've been having a difficult time dealing with him bringing men back to our dorm room. Any advice on how to deal with this?

-- *Steve, Boston College*

ANSWER:
First question, have you talked to your roommate about it?

We know it sounds like cheesy Dr. Phil advice, but as long as two roommates are communicating with each other, there's really no issue that can't be solved via some sort of compromise. Ok, sorry, that's not exactly true; sometimes a roommate really can be a stubborn, pig-headed jerk of such obnoxiously asinine proportions that you just want to rip their frickin' head off and piss all over their... oops, sorry, got carried away. Anyway, it doesn't sound like this guy is that bad; he just happens to be a horny gay guy.

Second question, have you thought about why it all bothers you so much in the first place? Because if you really don't have a problem with the homosexual part of it, then it really shouldn't be any different than a heterosexual roommate bringing girls back. So it's more an issue of common roommate courtesy (but to avoid being labeled as homophobic, you'd better be damn convincing when you tell your roommate it would make no difference to you if it was a girl he was bringing back and that it would still bother you the same). But assuming that's the case and the sexual orientation part has nothing to do with it, we'll stop there and direct you to our question/answer regarding *the sexile phenomenon* where we advise how to co-exist with a roommate (even if he/she is a player). It should be a few pages ahead, after the bathroom break.

-- The College Guy

QUESTION:

I recently started dating this guy. He's the greatest guy in the world and he's perfect for me. I'm positive that he's the one, but I also know that both of us are years away from thinking about marriage. So much could go wrong between now and then, so am I taking too big a risk if we start a serious relationship while we're still in school?

-- Ali, Syracuse

ANSWER:

It is NEVER a good idea to start a relationship already thinking about the future/end of that relationship. Do you think Kevin Federline thought it was going to work out long-term with Britney? Sometimes you just have to go with what feels right at the time. If it feels right now, then you should be together now. If you're still together in 5 years, then congratulations. If you're not still together in 5 years, then there will be a reason why you're not still together.

If he's as perfect as you say he is, then there is no good reason (assuming he's not gay) why you shouldn't start a relationship with him now. Don't deprive yourself of something good because you're trying to plan and strategize the best way to make him your husband years down the road (because we guarantee something will come up that ruins those plans -- You'll meet someone else, he'll meet someone else, you'll find out that he's your long-lost, separated-at-birth brother, etc.)

So you asked if you're taking too big a risk by starting a serious relationship with him. We think you're taking a bigger risk if you DON'T start a relationship with him.

-- The College Guy

NOTE FROM THE COLLEGE GUY:
The previous question tangentially touched on another topic that we feel is worthy of its own discussion...

Many people talk about a guy or girl being "the one" so we want to take a minute to talk about this perplexing phenomenon. We don't want to impose our personal views on the personal views (or religious views or philosophical views) of others but.... Wait a minute! What are we talking about? We've been imposing our views on others for years! It's our JOB! So if you don't want our views imposed upon your views, please stop reading... right... about... NOW!

Anyway, we think the idea of "the one" (short for "the one love of my life," "the one I'm meant to be with," "my one soul-mate," "the one Mr. or Ms. Right," etc.) is one of the most ridiculous idea out there.

Let's do some math. You would need to meet 50 new people (of your preferred gender) every single day of your life to give yourself even a 1% chance of finding your "one" match in this world of millions and millions of people. Oh, and you would have to live to be 1000 years old, just to get that 1% chance! And that's assuming that you would know instantaneously that he or she was your match (because there certainly wouldn't be much time left for second dates with all those millions of other people left to meet).

Anyway, people have these romantic ideas of finding their "one true love". They think it cheapens a relationship or the idea of love if you accept that there are many people out there with whom you could possibly be compatible enough for love to strike. It also helps people to get over a tough breakup to reason that he or she couldn't have been "the one" since [insert reason for breakup here] happened.

The cliché about there being "other fish in the sea" is cheesy, but true. Just because you catch one that might be perfect for you, doesn't mean that if he or she gets away you won't find another one just as good, if not better. We're not suggesting you settle for anything less than true love, but don't be naive enough to think that there is only one person out there in the world of millions (or even in your college of thousands) with whom you could fall in love and live happily ever after.

People are often afraid to commit if they think there could be something better out there. And they *should* be afraid to commit *if* they think they would act on impulses and desires to find out if someone else is better. But here's a newsflash for you: the reality is that you have to accept the fact that there will ALWAYS be someone better out there. Always. The thing about committed relationships (and eventually, gulp, marriage) is that you make the choice that you will not allow yourself to pursue those other people and you will only allow yourself to love the one whom you have chosen.

There are many people out there that you will be capable of falling in love with. Your search shouldn't be to find "the one" but rather to find "one of the ones" whom you are capable of falling in love with and then eventually committing to the idea of making him or her "the one for you", thus eliminating all the other potential ones out there that could have been.

-- *The College Guy*

Random Thought From AskTheCollegeGuy.com:

We love the fact that some of you are likely reading parts of this book while sitting on the toilet. And in just a few minutes, you're going to put this book down, unroll some toilet paper, and wipe your ass. That just makes us feel good. One minute you're reading our book, the next minute you're wiping your ass. That's fantastic!

But what if you *do* happen to be reading this book while sitting on the toilet? And what if you just realized there's no more toilet paper?!?!?!

Stay calm. Don't panic.

As always, AskTheCollegeGuy.com is looking out for you. We're leaving the next page completely blank. In an absolute emergency, feel free to rip the following blank page out of the book and use it to wipe your ass. We're not saying it's the ideal solution, and we're not saying it won't hurt like hell. But it's better than some of the messy alternatives, right?

Note: To find out why this page is blank, please read previous page.

Note: To find out why this page is blank, please read previous page.

Chapter Seven
-MARCH-

QUESTION:
I can never get into my room to study or sleep when I want to because my roommate always has her boyfriend inside. What should I do?

-- Sick of Listening to My Roommate
Gettin' Busy, Northwestern

ANSWER:
First we must make certain that everyone understands what it is we are talking about here. The situation you describe is more commonly referred to as the "sexile phenomenon". *[Actually it's usually just called "being sexiled" but AskTheCollegeGuy.com frequently adds the "phenomenon" tag to classify and sensationalize interesting situations, events, or trends commonly occurring on campuses throughout the country. These universal phenomena are part of what makes the college experience so similar for all college students, regardless of what institution you attend, and consequently keeps AskTheCollegeGuy. com in business.]*

The AskTheCollegeGuy.com Dictionary defines "Sexiled" as "being inconveniently barred from your room/apartment due to sexual activity occurring inside; the aforementioned sexual activity usually involves a roommate who is either drunk, inconsiderate, extremely horny, or some combination of the three."

The vast majority of problems associated with being sexiled can usually be fixed with a single conversation in which you explain to your roommate how you were inconvenienced. Ideally each roommate will realize that the room is to be shared equally and concessions can be made on both sides so that everybody's happy and neither of you are inconvenienced too greatly. Afterall, assuming you haven't taken a vow of celibacy and that you don't physically resemble a member of the Shrek family, the roles might some day be reversed whereby you get lucky and need some Love Shack privacy yourself.

It is suggested that ALL ROOMMATES come up with some type of signal to indicate when it might not be the best of times for others to enter the room. Locking the door should keep all non-keyholders from interrupting, so the signal is primarily to keep roommates from walking in on roommates. Some frequently used "sexile-in-progress" signs would be:

- ✓ A rubberband on the doorknob
- ✓ A secret code word written on a dry erase board
- ✓ Or the more direct approach of a post-it-note on the door saying something to the effect of "GO AWAY, I'M GETTIN' BUSY!"

Anyway, the bottom line is that you will get along much better with your roommate if you discuss these potential "sexile" situations before they arise and before they escalate to bitter feelings. Because, when you're hooking up, there's no worse mood-killer than banging on the door with shouts of "Open the door, bitch!"

                                        -- The College Guy

QUESTION:

I caught my boyfriend masturbating the other day and he told me it's no big deal and that all guys do it. Is that true?
                    -- Caught Him in the Act, Auburn

ANSWER:

We sent the AskTheCollegeGuy.com Research Team out into the field to do a very complex and scientific study to answer this question. After analyzing our data, we cross-referenced our results with the results of other reputable scientific studies on the topic of masturbation. The results of our comprehensive study yielded the following indisputable results:

- ✓ 96% of all college-aged males admit to masturbating.
- ✓ The remaining 4% are liars.
                              -- The College Guy

QUESTION:

Are internships valuable? Please explain.
                    -- Joan, University of Illinois

ANSWER:

Obviously this depends on what your future plans are. If you want to be the guy (or girl) who mops up the floor in an X-rated movie theater, then all the internships in the world probably aren't going to do a whole heck of a lot for you. But for most other areas - especially with the job market as tough as it is today - internships will certainly help give some substance to your resume and an edge in the interview process.

In a nutshell, the biggest thing about internships is that you can't expect too much. But here are some additional suggestions for things to keep in mind:

- ✓ You will not start at the top so don't go in with a chip on your shoulder even if you become somebody's bitch.
- ✓ The tasks you will be assigned could be boring, tedious, mind-numbing, or just plain shitty.
- ✓ Don't bitch and complain. Do everything with a big smile on your face and check all ego/attitude at the door.
- ✓ Network! Network!! Network!!! Meet as many people as you can. Make a good impression. Ask questions. But do NOT ask so many questions that you become known as that obnoxious, tag-along intern who never shuts up.
- ✓ If you're going to kiss ass, make sure it's not too obvious. And don't just spend your time trying to cozy up to or get noticed by the VP or CEO. Future hiring decisions are often made by lower level middle management. [Note: Even somebody's personal assistant or secretary could end up playing an instrumental roll in helping you land a future job, so be sure to practice equal-opportunity ass-kissing.]
- ✓ Always be thinking about your resume and what you're going to have to talk about in job interviews in the future. Look at the following for an illustration:

Joe A. Chiever

- ❖ G-Money Investment Bank, Junior Analyst, Summer 2004
- ❖ Johnson and Cooper Public Relations, Marketing Intern, Summer 2003
- ❖ Dewey, Cheatam & Howe Law Firm, Future Litigators of America training program, Summer 2002

Bob Slacker
- ❖ Lake Hottie, Life Guard, Summer 2004
- ❖ Wrigley Field, Beer Guy, Summer 2003
- ❖ Lazy Day Golf Course, Caddie, Summer 2002

All of Joe A. Chiever's summer jobs and internships were likely unpaid positions. Bob Slacker probably made several thousand dollars. We understand that financial constraints sometimes make it necessary to earn money for tuition or rent, but with the two resumes above, unless Joe College Student fails his criminal background check, we're fairly confident he's going to stand the better chance of getting most jobs he applies for that are looking for work experience.

One big thing to remember is that you don't always need to be with the biggest name company or working specifically for the head of the company. You never know where certain people or entire companies will be a few years down the road. For example, here at AskTheCollegeGuy.com and at our sister company RejectionHotline.com, we don't pay our interns a dime. But they're getting good experience to put on their resume. They're getting references and letters of recommendation. They're making good contacts. And they may see the real fruits of their labor in another year or so when AskTheCollegeGuy.com and The Rejection Hotline have firmly secured a hold on "Pop-Culture Phenomenon" status and are fielding offers to be bought out by Yahoo, AOL, Google, or that little kid down the street with the lemonade stand.

In short, it's all about gaining experience and making connections and having something to talk about headed into future job interviews. Internships offer a great way to do all of the above. So yes, internships can be extremely valuable.

-- The College Guy

QUESTION:

Should I stay in a relationship with a guy who just told me that a girl he dated is four months pregnant by him? We are not boyfriend and girlfriend - we just don't date other people when are both at school.

-- Danielle, Rutgers

ANSWER:

Partly because we didn't have enough information about the situation (i.e. what does he think about the fact that he fathered a child? is he actually going to be a part of this child's life? is he supporting the expectant mother? are they going to be getting back together?), partly because we didn't want to get pulled onto the Jerry Springer show with you when this whole thing blows up in your face (and if you're screwing around with the father of a pregnant girl's child, then chances are pretty good that it will blow up in your face), and partly because we have a really bad sense of humor... we decided to wait 5 months before answering your question.

Wait a minute...

```
  4 months pregnant
+ 5 months of us sitting on your e-mail
----------------------------------------------------------------
  That equals 9 months!!!
```

Ooops, looks like she already had the baby, you've probably long since made your decision, and we've been absolutely no help at all. Sorry about that.

-- The College Guy

QUESTION:

Last weekend me and 5 friends all had sex with the same girl and now I can't stop itching. My friends say they are itching as well. What can we do to stop the itching down there? She was so good though - why does this have to happen to us? all we wanted was a good time.

-- Friends Share Everything, UCLA

ANSWER:

Wow! [*Stifling laughter, stifling laughter, stifling laughter... regaining composure*]. Ok, first of all, we want you to go to your closet, reach in and pull out the box of porn you keep hidden in the very back. Pull out your favorite adult video tape and then.... repeatedly whack yourself in the head with it! Apparently, you and your buddies have foolishly mistaken videos like Gretta Gets Gang-Banged as a "how-to" video. But unfortunately, there's a big difference between professional porn stars and the special little lady who took turns with you and your buddies last weekend. Most of what you see in pornographic movies (especially the group stuff) involves porn stars who take frequent tests for sexually transmitted diseases. You and your buddies, on the other hand, seem to have found a dirty, frat-rat whore who probably doubles as a human petri dish for gonorrhea, syphilis, crabs, herpes, and any number of other things that might be the cause of your current itch-uation.

Now, we pride ourselves on being the optimistic, glass-is-half-full type of advice column, so we'll ignore the fact that you probably have every STD (Sexually Transmitted Disease) under the sun. Instead, we'll focus on the positive. Since you and all your friends have the same symptoms, maybe you can draw straws and only one of you will need to actually go to the doctor's office to find out what you've got and what you can do about it. Maybe you could all even split the cost of the appointment and the medicine, thus making your misery as cost-efficient as possible! Nonetheless, if friends really do share everything, as you say they do, you should all share in the humiliation of how your collective hormone-induced-shortsightedness likely resulted in the numerous dirty diseases that will haunt you for the rest of your lives. Share away boys!

-- The College Guy

QUESTION:
So -- If one nite u brought a guy that was 6 years older then u into ur room and he has a baby n he lives with hims babys momma n the baby n ur with him n one nite he was gonna go meet u some where n he didnt show up n he told u how much he LOVED U N MISSED U N HOW SORRY HE WAS n right after that he went n sleept with his babys momma , what would u do about that????????

-- Deans List Student, Harvard

[OK, so maybe we made up the "Deans List at Harvard" part because she didn't tell us her college]

ANSWER:
Well, golly gee, this is a real humdinger (*to be read like Ned Flanders from The Simpsons*).

From the sound of your e-mail, you seem like a very intelligent woman. We suggest you adhere to the following five-step program:

1. First, sit down with this fella and try to have an intelligent, civilized, rational conversation about the situation.
2. Midway through the conversation, have his baby's momma come join the conversation.

3. Get in a cat fight with his baby's momma - hopefully she'll call you a dirty ho-bag and a slut-face and you can call her a skanky-ass bitch.

4. Tell her, in no ambiguous terms, that "he my man now". If she says that "he her man and she gonna beat yo ass" than start trying to pull her hair out (if you can rip any of her clothing that's a bonus).

5. Go back to your life, forget about everyone involved in this situation, and look at yourself in the mirror and repeat the following: "I am an intelligent, motivated woman with big aspirations for my future... and I ain't gotsta take no shit from nobody."

And if our 5-step program doesn't work for you, we suggest you send your question straight to Jerry Springer.

-- The College Guy

QUESTION:
I was watching the movie "Road Trip" and wondered if you could give an overview of the rules to cheating?

-- Not so faithful, Florida State

ANSWER:
Obviously the phrase "rules to cheating" is pretty much an oxymoron in itself. After all, the very nature of the word "cheating" implies that you are ignoring and/or breaking some rule. Finding out that you've been cheated on can be one of the most painful experiences of a lifetime, so with very few exceptions, you are a dick (guys) or a bitch (girls) if you cheat on someone -- even if it was in a different zip code, area code, or time zone. It sucks so much that many people would rather be broken up with out of the blue than suffer the pain and embarrassment of being cheated on.

It is possible, generally in relationships based on insecurities, for weak excuses like "I was so drunk" to help you narrowly avoid losing your boyfriend or girlfriend. But even if all is forgiven and forgotten, post-cheating relationships should always be carefully examined by both sides because clearly there was at least something wrong, on one side or the other, before the cheating took place.

While cheating can never be condoned or encouraged, it should be noted that there are different situations in which cheating can take place and each situation can be evaluated/criticized differently (much like j-walking, shoplifting, and murder are all crimes - but clearly all 3 should be viewed and punished differently).

Cheating while drunk at a party
Chances of getting caught:
65% at a small school | 25% at a large school
Likelihood of the relationship ending if caught:
80%
Ranking on the AskTheCollegeGuy.com Bitch/Dick scale:
7 -- meaning 7 out of 10 people would consider you a bitch (girls) or a dick (guys) --

Cheating while drunk at a party where your significant other is also in attendance
Chances of getting caught:
95% at a small school | 85% at a large school
Likelihood of the relationship ending if caught:
90%
Ranking on the AskTheCollegeGuy.com Bitch/Dick scale:
8 -- meaning 8 out of 10 people would consider you a bitch (girls) or a dick (guys) --

Cheating with your significant other's friend, roommate, or sibling

Chances of getting caught:

45% if you both agree to keep it quiet | 75% if anyone else knows

Likelihood of the relationship ending if caught:

95%

Ranking on the AskTheCollegeGuy.com Bitch/Dick scale:

9 -- meaning 9 out of 10 people would consider you a bitch (girls) or a dick (guys) --

Cheating with your significant other's Siamese Twin

Chances of getting caught:

100%

If this happens, be sure to call Maxim or Cosmo (after e-mailing us) - it'll make for one hell of a feature story!

Cheating in a long-distance relationship

Chances of getting caught:

75% at a small school   25% at a large school

Likelihood of the relationship ending if caught:

50%

Ranking on the AskTheCollegeGuy.com Bitch/Dick scale:

5 -- meaning 5 out of 10 people would consider you a bitch (girls) or a dick (guys) --

Cheating with that too good to be true, once in a lifetime opportunity

Chances of getting caught:

Who cares?

Likelihood of the relationship ending if caught:

60%

Ranking on the AskTheCollegeGuy.com Bitch/Dick scale:

5 -- meaning 5 out of 10 people would consider you a bitch (girls) or a dick (guys) -- but if it was really too good to be true, the other 5 out of 10 will consider you a hero --

A few things that are NOT considered cheating:

* Masturbation - regardless of who you are fantasizing about - is not cheating. And if your significant other disagrees, please direct them to us and we'll straighten them out for you.

* Manually masturbating small fury woodland creatures for biological research does not count as cheating. *[Editors' Note: One of our interns, who is studying to be a veterinarian, asked about this one. We think he spends a little too much time in the lab.]*

* And finally, since the initial question referenced the movie Road Trip, we would be remiss if we did not remind people that your dog licking peanut butter off your genitalia also does not count as cheating. It makes you a f*cked up psycho in need of some major counseling, but it does not make you a cheater.
[Note: The "dog" mentioned above refers to an actual four-legged canine and does not refer to ugly people. If you convince an ugly roommate, professor, or pizza delivery person to lick peanut butter off your body, this is considered cheating and you can tell your psychiatrist that we said so.]

                                   -- The College Guy

QUESTION:
What up College Guy, my question is... what should I do if I have a grudge against the school mascot. Its not that I dont like him for no apparent reason but everytime I see that damn eagle he does something dumb like taps me on the shoulder from behind then walks ahead when I turn around like he didnt do anything. Should I fight him or what?
                          -- Why won't he leave me alone?!,
                              Georgia Southern University

ANSWER:

Are you in a room with padded walls right now? Just wondering. Anyway, we've got some bad news for you. At the risk of getting ourselves in legal trouble (like that school teacher who was sued for telling her 6-year-old students there's no such thing as Santa Clause), we're going to hit you with some shocking news. We realize this may be a preposterous suggestion, but what if, just WHAT IF your mascot isn't a real eagle? We know this might defy all logic, but what if it's actually just another student dressed up in an eagle costume? Further, it might not always be the same student. Further, it might even be, gulp, a girl in there!

Before you fight him, you might want to ask yourself a couple questions:

1. What if it's not a "him" at all? Despite what you may think, it doesn't require testicles or hairy legs to wear an eagle costume.
2. What if you fight "him" and lose? We can't think of many more embarrassing things than getting your ass kicked by Big Bird.
3. And speaking of embarrassing, are you really going to be proud of yourself if you beat the crap out of your school's mascot? Just remember, Randall Simon was the laughing-stock of Major League Baseball after his attack on the Italian Sausage during a human sausage race a few years ago at Miller Park in Milwaukee. *[Editors' Note: For those that didn't hear about this, Simon was lucky to escape criminal charges, but was cited and fined for disorderly conduct, for smacking the life-size sausage with a baseball bat. And yes, it did in fact turn out to be a girl inside the sausage costume.]*

-- The College Guy

P.S. Normally we never divulge e-mail addresses or any other contact information to anyone, for any reason. However, this guy freaks us out a little bit, so if we end up seeing an Amber Alert issued for a missing giant, stuffed eagle in the Southeast region of the United States, we're selling this guy down the river and turning his contact info directly over to the FBI.

P.P.S. If the Georgia Southern Eagle happens to be reading this... please, be careful!

QUESTION:
Why do all these guys I meet just want sex from me and not a relationship, am I not pretty enough?

                                          -- Confused, Arizona State

ANSWER:
If you've got "all these guys" wanting sex from you, it's likely got nothing to do with you not being pretty enough...

[Editors' Note: This question came in at 4:57 p.m. on a Friday and we're headed to a local bar for an AskTheCollegeGuy.com Happy Hour with free beer at 5:00, so we'll sum this up in one sentence so we can get out of here and call it a day.]

...maybe you just need to stop giving off that slutty, dumb-as-rocks, cheap-hooker, I'm-an-easy-score vibe. Good luck finding that relationship you're looking for!

                                          -- The College Guy

QUESTION:
I just got dumped by the only person I've ever been in love with. I can't eat, I can't sleep, I can't study. I just sit in my room and cry. I'm devastated and I don't know what to do.

                                          -- Help Me, UCLA

ANSWER:

First of all, let us commend you on remaining completely gender neutral throughout your question. It makes it slightly more difficult to answer your question when we have no clue as to your gender (or sexual orientation), but luckily this is a pretty general question with a universal theme.

So here are a few thoughts from the College Guy on breakups:

- ✓ NEVER easy. (And you need to accept this from the start so you don't start getting frustrated with yourself because you can't just forget about it and move on.)
- ✓ ALWAYS worse when you're the one who got dumped (especially if you didn't see it coming). If it wasn't your decision, then not only is your heart broken, but your pride, your ego, and your self-confidence usually take a beating too.
- ✓ ALWAYS worse when the breakup is with your "first love." It sounds cheesy, but this is the worst possible break-up because it will be almost impossible for you to imagine yourself ever having those feelings for anyone else again (excluding characters on The OC).
- ✓ The stronger your feelings for this person were/are.... the greater the pain of the breakup will be. Kinda like playing the stock market: the more you invest, the more it sucks when you lose.
- ✓ The fact is you're gonna be hating life for a while... but don't worry, because it definitely gets better (we promise).
- ✓ It HURTS (not as much as playing leap-frog with a unicorn, but it hurts).

- ✓ Listening to certain songs on the radio can be torture! [Note: It can also be therapeutic if you allow yourself to realize there are a ton of people out there (including the writers of those tear-jerking songs) who have been through exactly what you're going through -- and they were all able to make it through the tough times and bounce back. Even though it felt like it at the time, it wasn't the end of the world for the people who wrote those songs -- and it won't be the end of the world for you either.]
- ✓ It almost always helps to talk about it with somebody (a friend, a roommate, a brother or sister, your RA, etc.), especially somebody who has been through a similar situation before.
- ✓ It will take some TIME to get over it.... but... just remember that YOU WILL GET OVER IT!
- ✓ It happens to almost EVERYONE at some point in their lives.
- ✓ And it will probably even happen to you AGAIN.
- ✓ And just like the first time, you WILL get over it AGAIN (though the next time it won't seem so bad because you've been there before and you already know that it gets better).

-- The College Guy

P.S. Just so you know you're not alone, we feel obligated to point out that there are so many people in your situation, there's actually a holiday created just for you (and the millions of others in your situation). "Get Over It Day" is a new holiday taking place every year on March 9th (that's strategically selected as the mid-point between Valentine's Day and April Fool's Day). Get Over It Day exists, because EVERYONE has SOMETHING to get over...

GET OVER IT DAY – MARCH 9TH

Regardless of age, of race, or of gender,
If you're tall or short, if you're plump or slender.
If you're smart or dumb, if you're straight, gay, or bi-,
This day is for YOU, and we'll now tell you why.

Nobody is happy, every day of their life.
Not an American Idol nor a Desperate House Wife.
Not MVP athletes, nor Oscar-winning stars.
Not rich CEOs, nor hot chicks at bars.

We all have our issues; all lives contain stress.
At some point, we're all, an emotional mess.
Ex-boyfriends, ex-girlfriends, ex-husbands, ex-wives.
There are people to get over in everyone's lives.

Breakups, divorces, rejection of all kinds.
There's lots of bad [stuff] we can't get off our minds.
You miss him. You need her. You just want them back.
Sad, angry, depressed, you're all out of whack.

But as much as things suck, as bad as they get.
If you're fired from your job, if you're swimming in debt.
If you're aging or balding or get a cold sore.
Don't ever forget, that it could always suck more!

If you got your ass dumped, or you got cheated on.
It won't help to flee to Azerbaijan.
It's all part of life; it will help you grow stronger.
But this "pity party" of yours can't last any longer.

You can sit on your ass being sad and depressed.
Or you can choose to be strong, and do as we suggest.
March 9th is the day, to stand up and say:
"Screw that! It's done! It's Get Over It Day!"

- www.GetOverItDay.com -

Chapter Eight
-APRIL-

QUESTION:
How can guys say I love you soon after meeting you and
that they are madly in love with you and then a week later
just want to be friends??

> *-- Looking for Answers, Georgia Southern*

ANSWER:
There are lots of reasons that guys may say "I love you" and
not really mean it...

Maybe they just want to get you in bed.

Or maybe.... um... well.... maybe... uh... Ok, we tried to
think of other reasons, but we're sorry to report that the only
reason guys say they love you - under the circumstances
you described - would be get in your pants.

You didn't actually fall for this, did you?

> *-- The College Guy*

QUESTION:
hey I have this problem, ive been talkin to dis gurl over
da fone for quite a while, and just today she asked me if

I wanted to have fone sex. I said alright kool. but I never did it be4. she told me to start it off and I didint know what to do. I tried but she said that im not that good at it. so my question for the college guy iz "how do u have fone sex?"

-- Trying to Reach Out and Touch Someone,
Boston College

ANSWER:

Most AskTheCollegeGuy.com answers and advice are a collaboration of the whole AskTheCollegeGuy team (comprised of our staff writers and interns at colleges and universities across the country and our AskTheCollegeGuy. com Editors here at AskTheCollegeGuy.com headquarters *-- Editors' Note: If you're looking for a visual image of AskTheCollegeGuy.com headquarters, picture the Bat Cave, only not as cool*). Anyway... since phone sex is a very private and personal thing and one of our newest staff writers has been itching to share his phone sex story for a while, we decided to hand this question off to him.... So here it is:

Jay: OK, great question. And don't worry, a lot of guys are a little nervous their first time. But I think I can help you feel a little more at ease about the whole thing.... My "phone virginity" was taken like this:

Her: "Do you really want to do it?"
Me: "Yeah."
Her: "Um...OK."
Me: "Really?"
Her: "Yeah, but you have to start."
Me: "Uh...OK."
(silence)
Me: "Uh...ooooh."
(silence)
Me: "I wish...you...you're so...um...I'd like to..."
Her: "Yeah...?"

Me: "What?"

Her: "No, I was just saying 'Yeah,' like, cause I liked what you were saying…or…starting to say… never mind, just keep going."

Me: "Oh, good, OK."

(silence)

Me: "So... um... what are you wearing?"

Her: "What do you want me to be wearing?"

Me: "Um, I don't know... um... how about a big Panda Bear costume?"

Her: "WHAT? What the hell is wrong with you?"

Me: "Nothing! I was just trying to be creative... and romantic... and I thought it would be sexy."

Her: "Well there's nothing sexy about a big Panda Bear costume!"

Me: "Oh."

Her: "How about if I told you I'm completely naked, lying on my bed, rubbing massage oils all over my body..."

Me: "Wow!"

Her: "Ok, you take it from there..."

Me: "Oh, shit, I've got call-waiting. Hold on a sec."

(click)

(silence)

(silence)

(silence)

Me: "Ok, sorry, I'm back. That was my grandmother, but I told her I'm busy."

Her: "Ok, so I'm still naked on my bed with massage oils... what are you going to do to me?"

Me: "Um, ok... I'm slowly walking over to the bed..."

Her: "Yeah....?"

Me: "I'm running my hand underneath your shirt…"

Her: "My shirt? You idiot! I told you I was already naked!"

Me: "Oh, um, I meant, I ... um... I was just running my hand through your shirt on the floor."

Her: "What?"

Me: "Never mind... so anyway, I'm putting my hand..."
Her: "Yes..."
Me: "On your knee..."
Her: "Yes..."
Me: "OK. I'm sliding my hand farther up your leg..."
Her: "Yes..."
Me: "OK. I'm moving my hand... to your labia..."
(silence)
Me: "Do you like that?"
(silence)
Me: "Hello?"
(muffled laughter)
Me: "Oh that's real cool... you're laughing?"
Her: "I'm sorry... I'm sorry... but...
(more laughter)
Me: "What?"
Her: "Well.... LABIA???!!!??? I mean, honestly, who says that?"
(more laughter)
Her: "I gotta go..."
Me: "Ok, well, maybe we can try again another time?"
Her: "Uh, yeah, sure... whatever."
(Click)

Ok, so maybe that didn't actually answer the question about "how to have phone sex" but hopefully it has shed some light on the unasked question of "how NOT to have phone sex."
                                                    --The College Guy

QUESTION:
I'm a virgin and I'm ready to have sex with my boyfriend of 1 year. Do I tell him that I'm ready, or just surprise him and do it?
    -- Lil' Debbie, A small school in the middle of nowhere

ANSWER:
Woo Hoo!!! Finally!!! It's about time, you prude little nun-in-training!

(Just kidding)

So it sounds like you've made your decision and you should be commended for your decisiveness. After all, look at the facts. You're in college and surrounded by young men in their sexual prime. It would be a monumental waste to throw away such a first-rate resource. But seriously, one year is a long time to be in a relationship in college and it can be assumed that you and your boyfriend are pretty close at this point. So you should be able to tell him that you're ready. Telling him ahead of time can give you both time to prepare yourselves mentally (and physically if you need to buy condoms, shave or trim certain body areas, etc.) for the first time you do sleep together.

But on the other hand, if he knows it's going to happen, he might get nervous. This boyfriend of yours has pretty much gotten used to the routine of beating off to internet porn because he's been dating the Virgin Debbie, but now he's suddenly bombarded with the notion of pleasing someone else instead of just himself. Thoughts start racing through his head faster than Anakin's pod-racer; "What if I don't meet her expectations? It has to be perfect or she'll decide it's something she doesn't like to do and I'll never have sex with her again!" Before you know it, you're ready to seal the deal and he's so nervous that he pulls a "Limp-Dick-Louie" and can't get it up... So with all that in mind, maybe it's best not to tell him.

Go out, have a nice dinner, maybe see a movie (maybe a romantic comedy, or something else light or funny) and go back to your place. Once you're home and getting hot and heavy, tell him you want to do it... or better yet, just reach into the drawer of your night-stand and pull out a condom for him - he'll know what that means. This will deprive him of time to worry about anything except maybe a quick prayer that he doesn't reenact the Jason Biggs "premature ejaculation" scene from American Pie *[Note: Make sure this is NOT the movie you choose to watch with him before the big event.]*

And definitely don't get discouraged if it isn't amazing the first time either. You'll have plenty of time to improve. After all, perfection comes with lots and lots of practice!

-- The College Guy

QUESTION:
Why does it always seem easier to meet people when I'm drinking?

-- Social Drinking Dave, Oregon State

ANSWER:
Four simple explanations for why it is easier to meet people when alcohol is involved:

1. With alcohol in your system, you often don't care as much about what you're saying (the filter between your brain and your mouth tends to go on vacation).
2. With alcohol in their system, the people you're talking to often don't care as much about what you're saying either.
3. It provides an easy conversation topic and/or opening line:
   a) "Can I buy you a drink?"
   WARNING: Exercise extreme caution when using this line at a party with free drinks.

b) "Hey, what're you drinkin'?"
WARNING: Only use this line if the person is drinking from an unidentifiable cup or glass. You look like a moron if the words Budweiser or Amstel Light are clearly printed on the can or bottle.
c) "Holy shit am I wasted!"
WARNING: You run the risk of looking like a drunken fool with lines like this, particularly if the other person is sober. Also, NEVER use this line within the first hour of a party or immediately upon arriving at a bar.

4.   The 4th and final explanation for why it is easier to meet people when alcohol is involved is simple... "The Beer Goggle Phenomenon".

                                                    -- The College Guy

QUESTION:
I'm friends with this girl and she clearly has a severe eating disorder, but I really don't understand her because it's gotten so bad that she looks disgustingly thin. The thinner she gets, the worse she looks. Why do girls do that? And if I tell her that she looks gross, will that help?

                                                    -- Wants to Help, Emory

ANSWER:
Wait a minute, there are girls with Eating Disorders on college campuses? No way!
(OK, that'll be the only sarcastic comment in this response because clearly there's nothing funny about Eating Disorders and we're not going to trivialize the issue by trying to make this response witty or entertaining.)

But we're not going to ignore this question either because, as you probably know, Eating Disorders are a huge problem on college campuses across the country and what makes this issue more complicated than many other college social issues is that most people don't really understand how vast and complex the issue is. It's not just about food. It's not just about wanting to be thinner. In many cases there are serious psychological issues that go along with Eating Disorders. Low-self esteem, guilt, and shame are just a few of the emotions that can accompany an Eating Disorder. And to specifically comment on the question about the girl who looks "disgustingly thin," as hard as it is for us to comprehend, many people with eating disorders literally see themselves differently than we see them (and as you'll see from the passage below, it would probably be a bad idea to tell her she looks gross).

Since we don't claim to be experts on eating-disorders, we will pass on a short sample of advice from the S.C.a.R.E.D. organization (Support, Concern, and Resources for Eating Disorders)...

> *COMMUNICATE*
> *Try to talk to your friend or loved one in a gentle and loving manner. There isn't anything wrong with going to them and telling them you are worried and concerned about them. You can also let them know that you are there to listen if they want to talk about anything....*

(From someone who has battled an Eating Disorder)
> *"... people would make comments to me that only put me on the defensive, things like "You look like a skeleton". It hurt me and only made me feel worse. Like many with Eating Disorders, I suffered from low self esteem so these comments only made it worse..."*

The best thing you can do for yourself or anyone else battling an eating disorder is to contact professionals that are trained to help. Most colleges have counselors, dieticians, and other resources available through the Student Health department or the counseling center, and there are many online resources available as well, such as <u>www.NationalEatingDisorders.org</u>

Become informed so you understand the issues. Get help for yourself or be there for support for others.

-- *The College Guy*

QUESTION:
There's this guy that I thought I had connected with, but recently he totally turned the other cheek and I don't know why. I don't know him that well but we made out on several occasions. One night we were cuddling in his bed and I told him I'm a virgin and I wouldn't give him any. He told me that he thought I was beautiful and he really liked me. He asked if I wanted him to be my boyfriend. I said "I don't know" and I told him I never had a boyfriend before. But he said he still would like the job. He told me to page him later and I did but he never answered any of my pages. There was some drunken stuff at a party that I don't really remember a couple days later where I guess I made a fool of myself. But why would he say those things if he didn't mean it one bit? Well there's also at least one ex-girlfriend involved too. Could you please tell me what is going through his crazy mind?

-- *Hurt and Confused, Diablo Valley College*

ANSWER:
Right, because *he's* the crazy one, right? Ok, here's what we recommend... Pick up the phone. Call the admissions office

of your college. Ask them how it's possible that you got into college when you clearly left your brain back in High School.

Are you serious? You can't figure out why this guy doesn't want anything to do with you? Don't get us wrong, we're not saying that he might not be a dick, and we're not saying that you've necessarily done anything wrong (except maybe that "drunken stuff" where you "made a fool out of yourself" but "don't really remember it"), but what we *are* saying is that you sound a little naive.

Eventually, we hope to have an AskTheCollegeGuy.com radio show and this question would be perfect for that. We could ask you to repeat your story/question exactly as you sent it in and we could interrupt with our commentary to help you see things a little more clearly. We're not sure how well this will translate in print, but your original question will be **in bold**, and we'll interrupt (*in italics*) to point some things out to you...

There's this guy that I thought I had connected with, but recently he totally turned the other cheek and I don't know why.

We're about to give you half a dozen reasons. Keep talkin'.

I don't know him that well but we made out on several occasions. One night we were cuddling in his bed and I told him I'm a virgin and I wouldn't give him any.

What!? [mock surprise] You mean there might actually be a few guys out there who only care about sex? You said yourself you "don't know him that well" - so you don't think there's a chance he only wanted to get in your pants?

He told me that he thought I was beautiful and he really liked me.

He's thinking, "Maybe I can sweet-talk her into sex."

He asked if I wanted him to be my boyfriend. I said "I don't know" and I told him I never had a boyfriend before. But he said he still would like the job.

He's thinking, "The sweet-talk didn't work; maybe she needs the official 'boyfriend' label to go all the way."

He told me to page him later and I did but he never answered any of my pages.

He's thinking, "The sweet talk didn't work, the 'boyfriend' angle didn't play out, and I'm leaving here with blue balls." You're lucky you got his pager and not the Rejection Hotline.
[Shameless plug: www.RejectionHotline.com]

There was some drunken stuff at a party that I don't really remember a couple days later where I guess I made a fool of myself.

He's thinking, "Not only does she not put out, but she's a high-maintenance drunken psycho too."

But why would he say those things if he didn't mean it one bit?

By "those things" we assume you mean the whole "He told me that he thought I was beautiful and he really liked me" thing. As we've already explained, as unfortunate as this may be, there do exist some guys that will say anything to try to get a girl in bed. Most girls these days are smart enough to identify a player like that, thus rendering these smooth-talking posers ineffective. You, on the other hand, seem naive enough to be a good target. But lucky for you, it seems you're a strong-willed moral person whose virginal convictions are strong enough to rebuff these Jedi mind tricks. ["You're the only girl for me" sounds a lot like "These are not the droids you're looking for"]

Well there's also at least one ex-girlfriend involved too.

You've got to be kidding! So he's got an ex-girlfriend -- who he's probably still sleeping with. And you wonder why he's not returning pages from a nightmarishly-naive, virgin head-case that he barely knows?

Could you please tell me what is going through his crazy mind?

Um, we kinda just did... But, from where you're standing, we wouldn't suggest calling anyone else "crazy".

-- The College Guy

QUESTION:
Every day in biology, my teacher touches me inappropriately and tells me that's the way of life. He once, because his wife is infertile, tried to make me carry their baby. I don't know what to say. I think he really likes me, but I think I'm a lesbian!?

-- I've Got Issues, University of Colorado

ANSWER:
The second part of your question is completely irrelevant... We don't care if you're heterosexual, homosexual, bisexual,

asexual, or some kind of weird hermaphrodite with a fetish for small fury woodland creatures - what you've just explained is totally inappropriate behavior, especially for a professor.

Have you ever told your perverted prof that it makes you uncomfortable or asked him to stop? The whole "carry my baby" thing is a little too weird for us to fathom, so we're not sure if you're giving us the whole story or not. Regardless, if you don't want to become the story-line to a bad after-school special, we suggest you get some counseling and talk to a professional at your school about all this -- and while you're at it, figure out the whole hetero/homo thing. It'll make the rest of your college experience much more enjoyable if you're sure of your sexual orientation.

-- The College Guy

Chapter Nine
-MAY-

QUESTION:

What is with guys only wanting short girls? I'm short (5'2")
so I'm not complaining, but what's the deal?

-- *Cutie in Cali, UCLA*

ANSWER:

First of all, you're making a sweeping generalization and, to be
perfectly honest, we think you're very wrong about "all" guys
wanting short girls. You've obviously never hung out in a guys'
locker-room and heard comments (often lewd and sexually
explicit) about "the chick with the nice, tan, long legs."

While some guys are "breast guys" and some guys are "ass
guys," there are definitely a lot of guys who are "leg guys."

*[Important tangent/note to heterosexual girls everywhere on
behalf of heterosexual guys everywhere: Ladies, shave those
legs!!! If guys wanted to look at or touch stubble, they would
sit at home, stare in the mirror, and rub their own face all day!
Some guys can tolerate a girl's hairy legs (or armpits) better than
others, but there are plenty of guys out there – even your boyfriend
who might feel obligated to say it's no big deal – who will want to
run like Forrest Gump at the sight/touch of unshaven legs (even if
they say it's no big deal).]*

Anyway, since a lot of guys do like nice, tan, smooth, long legs, it's a safe bet that these *long* legs aren't attached to the bodies of *short* girls. Have you ever seen a short girl with long legs?

Cali Cutie, at 5'2", we're guessing you don't have long legs since that would probably mean you are missing a neck (so your ears rest squarely on your shoulders) and/or you have the world's smallest, most compact, torso. In either case, you'd probably look like you belong in the circus and not at UCLA.

Anyway, putting aside the reality of the situation (which is that guys actually like tall girls, short girls, medium-height girls, younger girls, older girls, blondes, brunettes, red-heads, smart girls, dumb girls… basically ANY girls!), we'll address the question that you asked, working under the assumption that your initial premise is correct.

So according to you, guys primarily want short girls. Ok, we can think of a few key benefits to short girls:

1. When walking side by side, a short girl would actually have to make a conscious effort to tilt her head *up* in order to catch her guy checking out other girls.

2. A guy preferring short girls might be working under the assumption that her hands, mouth, and, um, vaginal depth are properly proportional to the rest of her small body, thus increasing the chances that a certain body part *of his* will tend to look/feel much larger in comparison.

-- *The College Guy*

QUESTION:
So I went on a date with this guy on Saturday. My friends had always told me he liked me, but I wasn't sure. While we were at the doorstep he asked me to go to his Choir Concert on Sunday at 10am. I said yes, but told him to call me and remind me in the morning. He called me the next day at 8:30 am to make sure I was coming. I went but didn't get a chance to talk to him afterwards so I called him later that day to tell him good job. He invited me to lunch the next day. We went to lunch and then he asked me to hang out that night. Do you think this guy might like me?
-- Can't Read the Signs, University of Utah

ANSWER:
University of Utah, hunh? Guess they grow 'em pretty smart over there. OK, let's re-cap for a minute:

1. You went on a date with him Saturday night.
2. Your friends have been telling you that he likes you.
3. At the doorstep, he asked you to go to his Choir Concert the next morning.
4. You call him later that day and he invites you to lunch the very next day.
5. Then he asks you to hang out that night.

Well, well, well. This is a tough one. Normally we enjoy answering challenging questions and addressing difficult-to-read situations, but this one is doozie!
[Editors' Note: Doozie? Doozy? Doozey? We know it's not a real word, but we still want to know how to spell it!]

We exhausted all of our resources here at AskTheCollegeGuy. com Headquarters, but we still can't figure it out so we've decided to consult a more sophisticated online advice columnist to help us out with this one. We forwarded your question to <u>www.AskMyCousinTheSixthGrader.com</u> for further analysis.

-- The College Guy

P.S. In the meantime, you might want to pull your head out of your ass. Actually, forget that. Keep your head up your ass and try one of the following:

1. Get one of your friends to find him on the playground during recess and ask if he likes you "as a friend" or "more than a friend."
2. Pass him a note that says: Do you like me? Check YES or NO
3. This is only a last resort, but you might want to try (gulp!) actually talking to him about the situation. But start the conversation out slowly - try something like "I like chocolate, do you? I like the color red, do you? I like SpongeBob SquarePants, do you? I like you - do you like me?"

We'll let you know what we hear back from AskMyCousin TheSixthGrader.com

QUESTION:
I'm a frickin' senior in college!!! It seems like just yesterday that I was a freshman - why does it seem like college has flown by so much quicker than High School did?

-- Nostalgic Senior, Clemson

ANSWER:
Well, you mean other than the fact that you've probably been drunk, high, or otherwise incapacitated by mind-altering substances more of the time during college than in high school?

There's actually a perfectly logical explanation for why time seems to fly by in college (and no, we're not going to give you a cheesy expression about how "time flies when you're having fun" -- we put that right next to "the early bird catches the worm" and "if at first you don't succeed, try and try again" on our list of annoying clichés that should result in an immediate beating to anyone under the age of 65 heard using them).

This answer is going to be slightly out of character for us because it's going to be a completely serious answer, somewhat based on mathematics, and will be almost entirely lacking in sarcasm and cheap attempts at humor. BUT WAIT! Don't leave! Give this a chance, because if you think about it, it should make sense.... (and this also serves to address the e-mails from people who ask things like "why can't you guys ever just give serious answers to questions without always relying on your sarcastic humor for cheap laughs?")

Ok, here we go.... Let's figure you were around 16 years old in the middle of high school. And let's figure you were around 20 years old in the middle of college.

When you're 16 years old:
Your entire life, your entire world, and everything you have ever known and experienced is contained within a span of 16 years. So 4 years (of high school) is one fourth (or 25%) of that lifetime.

When you're 20 years old:
Your entire life, your entire world, and everything you have ever known and experienced is contained within a span of 20 years. So 4 years (of college) is one fifth (or 20%) of that 20 year lifetime.

So even though both high school and college are exactly 4 years in length, the perception will always be that college flies by quicker than high school because 20% (of your lifetime and everything you have ever known up until that point) will obviously seem like less than 25% (of your lifetime and everything you have ever known up until that point).

So a day, a week, or a year will always seem longer, the younger you are - and it will always seem to fly by faster, the older you get... (no wonder we needed recess and snack time so badly when we were little!)

-- The College Guy

QUESTION:

Why do they always put beautiful women on the cover of men's magazines? I think that's shameful. And isn't it the media and websites like yours that promote this exploitation of women?

-- Stacy, Wilmington College

ANSWER:

First of all, if you're offended by those magazines, you should check out the ones they keep behind the counter in the plastic-wrap! (or you can just check the box at the back of your dad's closet). Anyway, Stacy, you're entitled to your opinion - although we think it's shameful that you would call this shameful - but let's talk about your concerns for a minute or six. We're confident that we can not only convince you that it's not our fault, but we're gonna try to turn it around and show you that it's actually YOUR fault. So here goes....

Despite the fact that most college students snooze through their Intro Marketing class and manage to pass by simply reading the chapter summaries and throwing out buzz words like "demographics" and "target market," there is actually an entire industry out there consisting of marketing professionals. These are the people who get paid lots of money and spend lots of money doing market research so that they can prove, statistically and indisputably, things that AskTheCollegeGuy.com could have told them for free. For example:

1. Males like to look at scantily-clad attractive females.
2. Females like to look at scantily-clad attractive females too!

Ok, we can hear Stacy and all her girlfriends out there screaming "that's sooooooo not true!" But come on now, let's be honest. You know you enjoy thumbing through that Victoria Secret catalog, right? Well, how many (straight) guys do you know that would get the same enjoyment flipping through "Tighty-Whitey Weekly" or "Boxer-Briefs Illustrated"? That's right, guys would rather saw off their leg with a rusty butter knife than look at scantily-clad dudes.

[Editors' Note: This column originally ran a couple years ago, so some of the celebrity references might be a little out-dated, but you'll still get the point.]

As you may know, the magazine-of-choice at AskTheCollegeGuy.com headquarters is Maxim and a quick search through recent issues strewn about the office show recent cover-girls including: Anna Kournikova, Gina Gershon, Jessica Alba, Shannon Elizabeth, and numerous other hotties who could melt an igloo by simply ringing the doorbell. But before any of you Women's Studies majors out there even think about criticizing Maxim for such (brilliant) decisions, a quick look at other popular men's magazines (FHM, Stuff, etc.) show recent covers to include

Carmen Electra, Daisy Fuentes, and Jenny McCarthy, so it's pretty much nothing but hot chicks across the board, er, newsstand.

[Special Note about Jessica Alba on the cover of Maxim's November 2003 issue: That girl was so ridicuhot, that we almost considered taking a staff field trip to see her in "Honey." But common sense eventually prevailed and we went out drinking instead.]

Anyway, our point - yes, we actually have one - isn't that you'll find scantily-clad hot chicks on the cover of men's magazines. No, that's a no-brainer that even those of you on academic probation would likely expect. Rather, our point is that if you look, you'll also find scantily clad hot chicks on the cover of WOMEN'S magazines too!

Since Cara and Michelle (our 2 female interns) weren't here at the time, we sent Intern Jason down to a local convenient store to do some investigative reporting on women's magazines.

[Note from Intern Jason upon his return: That's Bullsh*t! They sent me out to get a case of beer. I came up with the idea of checking out the Girly Mags on my own.]

[Editors' Note: Whatever, you're still just a little intern. Now go put those beers in the fridge.]

Anyway, Renee Zellweger was on the cover of Vogue and Britney Spears was on the cover of Glamour! And it's no different for Women's magazines we've never even heard of: In Style (Julia Roberts), Marie Claire (Julia Styles), and Self (Angelina Jolie). But, Stacy, somehow these magazines stay in business - and women keep buying them. Do these women's magazines exploit women too?

And this idea that "women are hot, guys are not" is held by teenagers too (and we all know that teenagers can be some of the trendiest, most fashion-conscious people in America). The cover of Seventeen featured Liv Tyler, Teen Magazine featured Kristen Kruek, and Teen Vogue had Katie Holmes. Only Teen People had a man on the cover (and that was Clay Aiken - so don't get us started on whether that really counts as a man)!

And it will come as no surprise that every girl/woman that we saw featured on the cover of a magazine that month was hot - with the lone exception of Oprah Winfrey, but she owns her own magazine so she's earned the right to put herself on the cover.

So anyway, because BOTH males AND females like to look at attractive females, it's a no-brainer for the marketing and advertising industries to use attractive females on magazine covers or to sell products, regardless of the gender of the primary target market.

Think about beer ads... The Coors Light Twins? The St. Pauli Beer Girl? The Miller Lite "Catfight" commercial (a poolside argument turns into a clothes-shredding, wrestling match between two women who end up in bras and panties)? We're not marketing professionals, but it simply wouldn't be that way if the numbers didn't show that both males AND females are buying the products being marketed this way. We're gonna go out on a limb and say that the number of beers consumed by our female readers in the last month will be a helluvalot higher than the number of Strawberry Daiquiris consumed by our male readers.

So, Stacy, if you're looking for people to blame for the "shameful" ways of society, you should probably hop down off your soapbox for just long enough to empty all the beer out of your refrigerator, throw out all your magazines, and take a good look in the mirror because your purchasing decisions and your money (or your daddy's credit cards) have a far greater effect on this "shameful" state of affairs than the mass media, the advertising industry, or a random entertainment/humor column like AskTheCollegeGuy.com could ever have!

                                                    --The College Guy

QUESTION:
My boyfriend just informed me that he wants us to take a break. He said he needs some time and space. So should I just wait around forever until he makes up his mind?

                                                    -- Kelly, Brandeis

ANSWER:
Should you wait around forever? NO. Should you wait around for a while? Well, if you really want to keep him as your boyfriend, then YES.

Some people will tell you that when he says he needs "time and space" then your relationship is definitely doomed. Others will tell you to hang in there, that things will still work out. Unfortunately, there is no easy way to tell which decision your boyfriend will come to. But there is clearly one way to increase your odds of getting him back and/or keeping him as your boyfriend.

This is a little more intellectual and academic than we like to get while answering a question, but let's think about this like a problem you might find in an Intro to Logic class or in the games section if you ever take the LSAT or GRE. We can logically play out the scenarios and see what option gives you the best probability of success (assuming that your number one goal is to work things out between the two of you and get back together).

1. You wait it out --- and he comes around and wants you back. [IDEAL]
2. You move on --- but then he comes around and wants you back.
3. You move on --- and he doesn't come back to you.
4. You wait it out --- But he doesn't come back to you.

The situation is going to be an emotional roller-coaster for you no matter what. But look at the big picture for those four basic scenarios, and decide which ones you could live ones and which ones would be eternally frustrating.

Basically, you've got everything to gain by giving him his time and space and waiting it out (because when he comes around and wants you back, everything is perfect and you live happily ever after). That's generally worth the gamble if the worst case scenario is #4 where you wait it out and he doesn't come around. In that case you've only suffered slightly additional losses of time, pride, pain, (and whatever you spend on a few pints of Ben and Jerry's ice cream).

The most under-rated part of this whole situation is the incredible difficulty in actually giving him the time and space he wants. To get him back, you need him to realize what he's missing. But the fact is that you can't miss something if it's never gone. As hard as it may be to do, you've got to grant him that time and space that he's asking for (no matter how much you want to talk to him 10 times a day to convince him that he's making a mistake). Keep your distance and give him an opportunity to miss you because you're only gonna push him further away if you try to pull him back before he's ready (and we highly advise taking his phone numbers out of your cell phone to reduce your chance of becoming a late-night "drunk dialer").

-- *The College Guy*

[Note: Girls definitely throw out the "I need some time and space" line just as much as guys do. So if you're a guy reading this and you're in a similar situation, just re-read the answer and switch all mentions of HE and HIM to SHE and HER and replace the Ben and Jerry's ice cream with a bottle of Jack Daniels or a case of Beast Lite -- We don't condone drinking your sorrows away, but history has shown that it does tend to happen.]

QUESTION:

I'm a sophomore girl and last year as a freshman I had the biggest crush on one of my professors. I'm not in his class anymore, so I've decided I'm going to go for it. But I don't know how to do it without seeming too forward?

-- *Lindsey, Western Kentucky*

ANSWER:

Hmmmm. So you're not asking if we think it's a good idea... And you're not asking if you could get in trouble (or if he could fired)... You're just asking how to approach the situation without seeming too forward???

Unless you see something that resembles Paris Hilton or Jessica Simpson every morning when you look at yourself in the mirror, we really don't think you have much choice other than to be at least semi-forward. You can't expect this professor to take the risk and attempt to initiate something with you -- even if he does know you exist. Put yourself in his shoes for a second. He doesn't want to come off looking like the "dirty-old-man" professor going after the college girls (regardless of your bra size or skirt length).

Please don't misconstrue this as us telling you to go for it (because we don't want to be responsible when this blows up in your face), but IF you're going to try to pursue it, we'd suggest just starting with your basic flirting. Stop by his office for Office Hours. If he's not your professor anymore this will be his first sign that you're interested in more than History, Math, Political Science or whatever other subject your prey may teach. Talk to him, see how his summer was, and begin with some SUBTLE flirting. [*Note from The College Guy: We realize we don't have to explain anything relating to "how to flirt" because it seems to be a natural gift that girls are born with -- a gift which often times results in flirting when they don't even mean to be. This is one of the things that drives guys crazy about girls and is a big part of what makes reading girls more difficult than reading Braille with gloves on. But that's another topic for another day --- and yes, we realize that girls can make the same claims about reading guys.*]

Anyway, stop by his office on a couple of occasions and slowly pick up the intensity on the flirting (you might even be so bold as to make a small joke or off-the-cuff comment about the "teacher-student relationship"). Based on how he responds (and/or how fidgety and uncomfortable he gets) you should have an idea of whether he would be up for exploring some extra-curricular activity with you.

Since you've already decided to go for it, I guess all we can say is "Good Luck." Oh, and we'd urge you to keep things as subtle and discreet as possible. College students tend to be way too gossipy, especially relating to something scandalous like this. But then again, some people don't care who finds out about their scandalous college behaviors -- so if anyone reading this has a really good hook-up story (a professor, your RA's boyfriend or girlfriend, your roommate's mom, the old lady who serves the food at the cafeteria) or any other scandalous stories, send them in for Volume II.

-- The College Guy

P.S. We don't know exactly what type of girl you are, but we have one more suggestion for you: Even though it works in the movies, we would NOT suggest an all-out seduction attempt on your professor where you casually slide your hand up his inner thigh or start blowing in his ear. While there's always the chance that it could result in whatever you're looking for, you've got just as good a chance of ending up with a Heisman-like rejection or even a sexual harassment suit for an unwanted sexual advance. Just be careful - you could be playing with fire.

QUESTION:
What do you talk about on the phone? I hear people say they were "on the phone for hours", but I can never think of anything to say. What do people talk about?

-- Nothing to Say, UVA

ANSWER:
Wow! Are you a decedent of Helen Keller? Or did you grow up locked in the cupboard under the stairs? All jokes aside, we will now teach you how to talk on the phone. [Well, maybe not "all" jokes aside.]

A typical phone conversation begins with something along the lines of "hello" or "hey" or "what's up" or, if you're feeling really daring, maybe a combination of two: "Hey, what's up?"

Usually people have a topic in mind or a question to ask when they call someone:

- ✓ Where do you want to go for lunch? for dinner? for spring break? for sperm/egg donations?
- ✓ I wasn't in class today. Could you tell me what was discussed, what the assignment was, or what the hot T.A. with was wearing?

Perhaps you are trying too hard to find something important to say. You don't always have to say something deep and profound. Some people just never have anything intelligent to say, but this is OK. Some people are meant to speak softly but carry a big stick.* Congratulations, you must be one of these people - so you might want to just shut up and not speak unless spoken to.

[Note: The "carry a big stick" expression was coined by the great Theodore Roosevelt. But it's OK if you didn't know that because you don't seem to bare much resemblance to him. You remind us more of Theodore Chipmunk (Alvin and Simon's brother).]

There's also a strong possibility that your telephonic conversation skills (and overall personality) will evolve and improve with time, as you get older. If this is the case, we recommend you either crawl into a hole and hibernate until you grow a personality or find out if your school has a program for mimes.

-- The College Guy

QUESTION:
I really really like this girl in my film class, but she's definitely out of my league. I try not to think about her, but she lives in my dorm and I see her all the time. I know I don't have a shot with her, so what should I do?

-- Bobby, NYU

ANSWER:
Film class, hunh? Ok, we'll speak to you through the language of film (and some of our favorite movies of all time) to show you that anything is possible...

IF a bare-footed, hung-over John McClain can single-handedly foil the plans of Hans Gruber and all those terrorists who seized the Nakatomi building in Die Hard...

And **IF** little Danny Kaffee can simply demand "the truth" and convince Colonel Nathan R. Jessep to admit that he ordered the Code Red in A Few Good Men...

And **IF** a "5-foot-nothin', 100-and-nothin'" Rudy can sack the quarterback on the last play of the game for Notre Dame...

And **IF** a rebellious Harvard janitor can solve complex combinatorial mathematical equations in Good Will Hunting...

And **IF** the fat kid in Old School can survive the face-plant (with a cinder block tied to his yoo-hoo)...

And **IF** the little kid in the Sixth Sense can really see dead people... *[Note: He wasn't getting his ass kicked by the other kids, because he was different, it was because he was a boy with the name Haley!]*

And **IF** a radioactive spider-bite can turn a dorky little photographer like Peter Parker into a stud superhero capable of landing Kirsten Dunst...

And **IF** a fat-ass, ugly green troll named Shrek can score Cameron Diaz (albeit in cartoon-form)...

…then maybe ***even you, Bobby,*** can get your dream girl!

-- The College Guy

P.S. OK, so maybe all of the above is Hollywood magic and in real life you don't really have a shot in hell of getting this girl (after all, there's gotta be a reason why you were so sure she was out of your league in the first place). But think about it this way, other than a little pride, do you really have anything to lose by giving it a shot? As long as the possible rejection won't cause you to flip out and lose your grasp on reality (something like John Cusack in High Fidelity), then go ahead and give it a shot. Start talking to her, get a sense of what kind of girl she is and what she thinks about you. Then, if you see even the slightest interest on her part, ask her if she'd want to study together, grab some lunch, or (hello! film class?) go to a movie some time.

Optimistic Conclusion: Remember, you miss 100% of the shots you don't take!

Realistic Conclusion: Remember, if you think she's out of your league, be prepared to find out you're right.

Chapter Ten
-JUNE-

QUESTION:
I was wondering if you have any advice for living with a roommate of the opposite sex. I'm a girl and will soon be living with a guy. A lot of people are telling me they think we'll hook up, etc. but I think that would be really weird. I want to insure that we keep our roommate relationship totally platonic and happy, so what's the easiest way to tell him that I'm not interested in being anything but roommates and friends?

-- Roxy, Colorado State University

ANSWER:
Well, probably the easiest way to tell him that you're not interested in being anything but roommates and friends is to say "Hey, I'm not interested in being anything but roommates and friends."

But seriously, just don't get into the "mixed signals" department. Make sure your body language isn't sending a different message than you're intending him to receive. If you have a tendency to be flirty or touchy-feely with guys, make a conscious effort NOT to do so with this guy. Have guys over, talk about your boyfriends or other guys, and treat him like one of your girlfriends -- unless of course you have a tendency to prance around naked with your girlfriends.

But remember, horny/desperate/interested guys will interpret *anything* you say or *anything* you do to mean "maybe she's interested in me". Try to stay away from comments like "wow, I wish I could find a guy like you" or "wow, you look really good tonight". You don't want this guy mistakenly thinking he makes you hotter than the stash of naked Brad Pitt photos you keep under your bed. *[Editors' Note: As soon as "naked Brad Pitt photos" was mentioned, one of our female writers immediately began getting fidgety in her chair, excused herself from the room, and came back seven minutes later looking extremely disheveled and flushed in the face. We're not really sure what that was all about, but as soon as she returned, she asked for a cigarette.]*

Anyway, moving on from the personal habits of our female staffers, if all else fails and you really want to make sure he doesn't think of you as more than a friend, you might want to try some combination of the following drastic measures to gross him out:

- ✓ Let him see you shaving your armpits.
- ✓ Wear shorts around the house when you haven't shaved your legs in a really long time.
- ✓ If you're in the room when he's watching baseball, yell "touchdown!" when you see a homerun.
- ✓ If he's watching football, say "Oooh, that meanie looked like he was trying to hurt that nice boy running with the ball."
- ✓ Occasionally "forget" to flush the toilet after taking a huge dump.
- ✓ If you're ever hanging out alone with him, make sure you have Mexican food with lots of beans for dinner and then fart away! The louder and smellier, the better.

✓   Keep all your sexy underwear hidden from view, but occasionally leave a pair of big 'ol granny panties lying around [extra points if they've got shit stains].

If all that still doesn't work, then we can't help you because it looks like you've got yourself a genuinely-obsessed, creepy-psycho-stalkerish-wannabe-boyfriend living with you. Good luck!

-- The College Guy

P.S. If you really try all the above measures and this guy STILL wants you, then you must be DAMN hot and you should ditch the obsessed roommate and move into the extra bedroom at AskTheCollegeGuy.com headquarters.

QUESTION:
OK, I am very sexually attracted to girls when I'm drunk and I often "check them out", but I would never want a relationship. Am I Bisexual?

-- Not Sure About Things, University of Georgia

ANSWER:
Ok, this is a very difficult question to answer. We need more information. Our suggestion is for you to buy a video camera or web-cam, act on these impulses the next time the opportunity presents itself, and be sure to record the entire thing from beginning to end (including foreplay and any post-relations cuddling). Send us the tape and our AskTheCollegeGuy.com Sexperts will evaluate the scenario and let you know if you are actually bisexual.

--The College Guy

QUESTION:
My damn professor screwed me with my final grade! I had an A on the mid-term and an A on the Final and I got a B in the course. Any advice?

-- B-Listed, Michigan State

ANSWER:
At the risk of overlooking a potentially very simple answer to this question, we have to ask a couple of simple/obvious questions:

- ✓ Have you taken a look at your syllabus? If your final grade is also based on class participation or attendance, then that might have been what did you in ... of course, you were probably absent the day the syllabus was handed out so you wouldn't really know anyway.
- ✓ Have you talked to your professor about it yet? It could be an honest mistake by an absent-minded professor.

If you've checked your syllabus and talked to your professor, and you still feel like you got screwed.... well.... guess what? You probably did get screwed and it sucks to be you!

Better luck next semester, but in the meantime, take a look at the following and see how many pertain to professors at your school.

"When Professor says this... They really mean this!"
Written by John H. Bickford, Jr. (c) 1996.
Copyright (c) 1996 by John H. Bickford, Jr.

Professors Say: This needs some minor revision.
Professors Mean: *I never actually got around to reading it.*

This won't be on the test.
Nap time!

I'm not fully up to speed on that.
I've got my head up my ass.

Not much is known about . . .
I don't know anything about . . .

We'll be spending a fair amount of time on this important concept.
This was my dissertation topic.

Talk to the department secretary.
Piss off.

Talk to me in my office after class.
Get out of my face.

There are two TAs available to help you.
I can't be bothered.

This year I'll be scaling the grades.
I just passed tenure review.

Let's break up into quiet discussion groups.
I have a hangover.

Let's have class outdoors today!
I had beans for lunch.

Well, that answer would be beyond the scope of this course.
I haven't a clue.

Hmm . . .
What the fuck?

Please note the last day to withdraw.
The midterm's gonna suck.

The tests will all be multiple-choice.
I take questions directly from the study guide and have grad students do all my grading.

Don't come in late during my lecture.
I have the attention span of a fruit fly.

Save your questions until the end.
I have the attention span of a retarded fruit fly.

The final will be comprehensive.
I'll expect you to recapitulate in two hours everything I couldn't fully cover myself in 15 weeks.

Ten percent of your grade is based on class participation.
I'll be fudging your grades.

Everyone will prepare in-class oral presentations.
This course is outside my specialty--I'll just bluff it and let YOU teach.

I haven't had a chance to make up the syllabus for this course yet.
The department chair stuck me with teaching this course at the last possible minute.

Well, it was on the syllabus.
I'll hold you responsible for this even though I forgot about it myself.

We'll just skip the term paper this semester.
There wasn't enough in the budget for a TA.

Bring a number 2 pencil to the exam.

There wasn't enough in the budget for a TA.

Attendance is required and will be counted in your grade.
I'm so boring that no one would show up otherwise.

Read chapters 5 through 10.
I'm not coming in at all next week.

We'll have to cover this chapter quickly.
I screwed up the lecture schedule.

Let's go over the exam.
Half of you failed.

It was in the textbook.
I pulled it out of my ass.

I'm postponing today's exam.
There's stuff on the exam I forgot to cover.

Don't write on the question sheet.
I'm so lazy I just use the same exams every semester.

Next time we'll see a film.
I ran out of lecture material.

"When Professor says this... They really mean this!"
Written by John H. Bickford, Jr. (c) 1996.
Copyright (c) 1996 by John H. Bickford, Jr.

-- The College Guy

QUESTION:
I am in college and I have never frenched a guy before! It's pathetic I know, but I guess the timing was never really quite right, or the feelings were just never there. Anyhow, I am with someone right now, and I know that we will french kiss in the near future. But I am really nervous! Of course, I've seen it on TV, and have even watched some of my friends, but I still have no idea how to react if he tries. I need your help. Can you please explain to me how to french kiss?

-- Needs Some Practice, Kenyon

ANSWER:
We highly suggest you rent the movie Cruel Intentions. And we're not just suggesting that because the scene with Sarah Michelle Gellar on Ryan Phillippe's lap is the most erotic scene in movie history in which no clothing is removed. The film contains a great "How To French Kiss" scene in which Kathryn (played by Sarah Michelle Gellar) teaches Cecile (played by Selma Blair) how to kiss.
[Note: This scene was so good that it was later spoofed (disgustingly yet hilariously) in Not Another Teen Movie.]

But in case you don't get a chance to rent our movie suggestion (or in the event that you keep yourself so innocent and pure that you won't allow yourself to watch a Rated-R movie), we'll give you the College Guy's Forbidden Five:

1) Bad Breath (as terrible as bad breath is to smell when you're close to someone, it's even worse to taste when you're kissing someone)

2) Too much tongue (Woah, relax! There's no prize for getting your tongue all the way down your partner's throat. Mix it up a little, keep your tongue in your own mouth part of the time, and try kissing gently with the lips some of the time)

3) Too much slobber (If either of your faces are covered in saliva during or after, there's a problem)

4) Illegal Use of the Teeth -- 5 Yard Penalty (A little nibble here and there is ok, but pain or blood indicates you've gone too far)

5) Pay Attention to what you're doing! (Eyes should usually be closed while kissing, but that's a matter of personal preference. However, if you do choose to keep your eyes open, it shouldn't be to watch some over-the-shoulder television. Guys, unfortunately this includes Sports Center.)

-- The College Guy

QUESTION:
I've had a long-distance girlfriend for almost a year now. I definitely love her, but the distance thing is killing me and every time I go out I'm tempted by other girls. Is that normal?

-- Kevin, University of Kansas

ANSWER:
Ahhhh, the long-distance relationship question. The second-most common college predicament of all time. [The most common college predicament of all time is "Should I go out drinking tonight or should I stay in and study?"] Unfortunately, unlike the drinking/studying dilemma, there is no simple answer to the long-distance relationship issue, and everyone will have a different answer for you:

- The Scientific Answer: Your body is constantly producing testosterone (if you've never heard of testosterone, you're not really in college yet, so get your ass off this website). It is this hormone which causes you to have feelings and urges toward girls you find attractive -- so yes, it is completely normal. Of course, adding alcohol or any other mind-altering substance into the mix makes it increasingly difficult to control yourself and you may start thinking with, um, the wrong head.

- <u>The Typical Guy Answer</u>: Dude, are you crazy? Get drunk, hook up, and have fun! What she doesn't know can't hurt her. Besides, it's not cheating if she's in a different area code. And if you do get caught just blame it on being drunk and say you blacked out.

- <u>The Typical Girl Answer</u>: Being able to resist sexual temptation is a true test of the love you have for your girlfriend. Don't give in. Besides, if you really loved her, you wouldn't even notice the other girls. [*Note from the College Guy: refer to the Scientific Answer above if any girl gets you to question even for a minute that you shouldn't even notice other girls.*]

OK, the above 3 answers should illustrate our ultimate point (which you've probably already figured out if you've tried discussing this with any of your friends) and that point is that everybody you ask will have a different answer (maybe not to the extremes illustrated above, but different nonetheless). Unfortunately, nobody else (the College Guy included) can tell you how to handle the situation because nobody else can know the specific dynamics of your relationship or the depth of your feelings for each other.

Certainly there are some long-distance relationships that are meant to last (which would lead to the thinking that you should resort to cold showers or masturbation to keep from jeopardizing such a relationship). On the other hand, a much larger percentage of these relationships are doomed for failure and will end at some point in the near future regardless of whether you cheat or not. Only you can know for sure how strong your feelings really are for this girl, where the relationship is heading, and whether it's worth the risk of losing her.

Try asking yourself some of the following questions which we like to call The Long-Distance Litmus Test:

1. If you remain faithful and then somehow end up breaking up much later on, are you going to regret the fact that you remained faithful and passed up opportunities with other girls?
2. If you decide to allow yourself to cheat on her and then you end up breaking up (which, based on history, will most likely end up happening if you cheat), are you going to regret your actions when you realize that they led directly or indirectly to the end of the relationship?
3. a) How would you react if you found out she had cheated on you?

    b) Are you OK making her feel that way?
4. Which is more important to you: Keeping her as your girlfriend or being free to do whatever you want with your college experience?

Not easy questions, but your honest answers to these questions should give you a better idea of what to do. Keep us posted on how it turns out. *[Note: College Guy's odds are 50-1 that you're broken up by the time this book gets published. Actually, who are we kidding? Odds are only 3-1 that this book will even BE published.]*

--The College Guy

QUESTION:
Dude, this website kicks ass! Keep doin what your doin cuz your my freakin hero!

-- *Stoner, The Ohio State University*

ANSWER:
Thanks, Stoner. We really appreciate the ass-kissingly kind words. Your e-mail was truly heart-warming.
[Note: There is a fine line between "heartwarming" and "heartburning"... Kindly-worded e-mails = heartwarming; 7 Beast Lites, 5 bean burritos, 3 tequilla shots, and a meat-lovers pizza = heartburn.]

Clearly we don't keep AskTheCollegeGuy.com going for the money. At last check, our bank account showed a balance of $12.37. Sure, we've got pipe dreams that help keep us going (this book making the New York Times Best Seller's list, our column running regularly in Maxim, Lindsay Lohan applying to be our intern), but it's really our fans, and the faithful support that you show us, that truly keep us motivated. And it means even more coming from a self-proclaimed stoner like this guy from Ohio State.

So you might wonder where we're going with all this. That's a fair question since most of the time we don't even know where we're going with half the crap we write. But we're actually focusing on Stoner's comment that we are his "freakin hero!"

Everyone needs a hero, a role model, someone to look up to, someone to emulate, someone to aspire to be like. Britney had Madonna. Paris Hilton had Pam Anderson. The OC had 90210.

So we figured it was about time that we found our own officially-designated hero, our own role model. Here are some of the names that were thrown around AskTheCollegeGuy. com headquarters:

The editors at Maxim?   No. While we're a big fan of the magazine and we'd love to get them to run our column someday [hint, hint], they still refuse to return our calls.

Will Ferrell?   No. He's clearly a comic genius, but we're haunted by the image of his bare ass running down the street naked in Old School.

The Rejection Hotline guy?   No. That would be too narcissistic and self-serving because, as some of you may know, he's actually one of our bosses too.

The guy in the Paris Hilton sex tape? No. We want a hero that's one of a kind. That guy just happened to be lucky that the she hit "night vision" instead of "off".

Steve Bartman?   No. We're not from Florida and we really don't care that the Marlins won the World Series in 2003. Plus, he kinda looked like a dork - or at least that's what the thousands of people who dressed up like him for Halloween that year made him look like.

And then it came to us...

We hereby officially declare the newly anointed hero of AskTheCollegeGuy.com is Bill Simmons.

More commonly known as "The Sports Guy," Simmons is a columnist for ESPN.com's Page 2 and ESPN The Magazine. With a witty combination of sports knowledge, pop-culture references, and a smooth, easy-to-read, humorous writing style, The Sports Guy is arguably one of the best writers of his time.

[Editors' Note: For those expecting our standard sarcasm or a hidden agenda for such apparently ass-kissing remarks, you won't find it. We've been reading this guy's stuff for years and we genuinely mean every word.]

Very Important Note: Unlike the Madonna/Britney relationship, there will be no making out between The College Guy and The Sports Guy - although we did exchange a drunken high-five at the Super Bowl in New Orleans a few years ago.

-- *The College Guy*

Chapter Eleven
-JULY-

QUESTION:
I luv you, college guy. Will you marry me? I'm pretty hot (and pretty desperate too).

-- Lizzie, a prestigious Ivy League school

ANSWER:
Let's make sure we've got this right... you say you're "pretty hot" but you're also "pretty desperate"? What?! [To start off the Double-Jeopardy round, we'll take "contradictory ideas that make no sense" for $400, Alex.]

You had us running to meet you at the alter right up until the "desperate" part. Unfortunately, "desperate" isn't exactly tops on the list of characteristics most people look for in a potential spouse, so we're going to have to decline your marriage proposal (but send in a picture and we might invite you down for a one-night, drunken romp at AskTheCollegeGuy.com Headquarters).

-- The College Guy

P.S. While "desperate" isn't necessarily a quality people look for in a potential spouse, if you're just looking for a little action or a one-night stand, then you're definitely marketing yourself the right way. If you walk into a bar, pick out a random, heterosexual, single guy and whisper "I'm pretty desperate" in his ear, we're betting that you'd score with 86% of them. The remaining 14% will be too busy looking around for the hidden cameras.

QUESTION:
Why are all guys such jerks?

-- Joanna, University of Georgia

ANSWER:
[Editors' Note: It's so refreshing to have both male and female AskTheCollegeGuy.com staffers. We're going to let some of our interns take a stab at this one.]

Perspective Of Our Female Interns:
It has yet to be documented in any medical journal or scientific studies that *jerkiness* is a dominant trait in the male gene structure, so for the sake of argument, we'll assume that guys actually can control the release of their inner-jerk.

Many guys just don't know any better. They've been getting away with certain behavior for so long (often times still getting whatever girl they want), so what's going to motivate them to change? Nothing. Not unless something is done about it. We need to stage a jerk-boycott! We must unite every college girl in the country to adopt a zero-jerk-tolerance policy! At the first sign of jerk tendencies, kick that guy to the curb. Actually, let's take it a step further. It is hereby declared, no sex for any college guys until...

*[**Editors' Note:** Woah, woah, woah... settle down, relax, take a midol. Sorry ladies, we here at AskTheCollegeGuy.com are all in favor of free speech and we think censorship is a terrible, terrible thing... but c'mon, let's get serious. Ok, we're turning the column back over to our female interns to finish the Female Perspective*

on this question, but you'd better cut the sh*t with this anti-male propaganda or we'll lose half our readers!]

Ok, unfortunately it is also partially the fault of us girls. *[Editors' Note: Ah, now that's better.]*
We girls are not nearly doing our job in making it clear as to how we should be treated. College girls seem to think that when we put on make-up, tight little outfits, and walk around in a ditzy drunken stupor at frat parties, that guys will take us seriously and treat us with respect. That is simply not true. And then we get pissed when they act like jerks.

You don't have to get mixed up with every guy who shows you some attention, throws a smile your way, buys you a beer, and maybe accompanies it with a cheesy line or two. You have to be selective. You can't complain about having hooked up with a jerk if you didn't get to know him before you let him in your pants. If you get to know him first, you can eliminate the jerks before you become too vested in the relationship. Bottom line is that you're going to be treated the way you allow yourself to be treated. If you carry yourself with confidence and class, then guys will feel the need to step up their game before they even approach you. If more girls would require more from the guys they "hang out with," then these guys would get the picture and you'd see more of their good qualities rather than that ugly inner-jerk. Much like dogs, guys must be trained!

On a slightly different note, part of the whole guy/jerk phenomenon is due to girls who pass over the genuinely nice guys to go for Joe Popular and Mike Hottie instead.

Perspective Of Our Male Interns:
Why are guys such jerks? What? Guys aren't jerks... shut up, you don't know what you're talking about.

                                    -- The College Guy Interns

QUESTION:

All I want to do is have an orgasm. I don't want to have sex though. Is there any ways that you know a girl could get off, I mean really get off, besides masturbation???

-- *Horny Virgin, University of Washington*

ANSWER:

So you don't want to have sex. And you don't want to masturbate. But you want to "really get off." Well it sounds like you're in quite a pickle! And speaking of pickles...... actually, never mind, scratch that - the pH balance of the pickle juice might not be such a good idea down there anyway. And regardless, the use of pickles, cucumbers, or undersized watermelons would all probably still be considered masturbation and you've already ruled that out.

So, with sex, masturbation, and the left side of the produce isle ruled out, you're going to have to find another person who would be willing to help you out with your situation. There are many things besides sex that people can do to get each other off. Have you ever had a boyfriend? Have you ever hooked up with a guy (over the age of 16)?

If you find the right guy (which could be *any* guy with a working knowledge of the female body, the drive and motivation to accomplish a goal, a 12-months subscription to *Maxim* magazine, and maybe a flashlight or spelunker's helmet), you won't have to worry about how to "really get off" -- because that becomes *his* responsibility. All you have to do is give him a little guidance as to what feels good and what doesn't.

-- *The College Guy*

P.S. If this doesn't work, you can contact one of our former AskTheCollegeGuy.com writers to help you out. His name is Joel, he's devilishly handsome, his e-mail address is joel@noitcejer.com, and his phone number is 617-861-3962. He'll be waiting!

QUESTION:
What's the hardest part about college?
                    -- Soon To Be Freshman, Texas Tech

ANSWER:
You mean other than the pavement that you'll hit the first time you trip and fall while stumbling home drunk from a fraternity party?

Anecdotal drunken injuries aside, this is a tough question to answer because it varies so drastically from person to person. For some people, the hardest part about college is the academic workload. For some, it's making it to class in the first place. Some struggle to fit in socially. Others will battle homesickness, depression, eating disorders, drug problems or a veritable plethora of other serious issues. So while we can't claim to know the one absolute "hardest part about college," there is one big universal beast that will rear its ugly head in some form or another to most college students at some time during their college careers...

This beast (having nothing to do with Milwaukee's Best beer) is better known as "Time-Management." But hold on! Wait just a second before you start muttering something about how we sound just like your parents, teachers, and late-night infomercials. Yes, we know you've probably heard about time-management before from the adults in your life whose advice you habitually tune out the second the words escape their 50-something-year-old lips. But hopefully you won't use the same deaf ear to listen to us that you usually reserve for "adults" who "don't know what the hell they're talking about."

Anyway, learning to efficiently manage your time really is a crucial skill, both for college and for life in general. Yet so many people struggle with it (AskTheCollegeGuy.com staff included – as evidenced by our periodic lapses in timely website updates and the fact that production of this book is about two years behind schedule).

Anyway, most schools have free time management classes or workshops you can sign up for. And unless you're a detail-oriented, anal-retentive, obsessive-compulsive, palm-pilot-wielding freak who is on time for everything, never wastes time, and doesn't know the meaning of the word "stress," we sincerely recommend you take some kind of time-management class or workshop. You've probably got more free time now then you ever had in High School (remember, back when you were in class for something like 7 or 8 straight hours??!!!??). But if you want to successfully balance the fun college stuff with the not-so-fun college stuff – at least well enough to stay afloat academically so you make it through to each subsequent semester – you're going to have to battle many time management issues along the way.

By the way, this question/answer is a perfect example of why we consider ourselves to be more of an "entertainment column" than an actual "advice column" and usually steer away from most serious topics. We can tell you all about how important time management is and we can advise you to take a time management class, but come on, the reality is that 98% of you are reading this thinking "I don't need to take a stupid time management class" and you're probably not going to be convinced otherwise by some patronizingly condescending advice columnist.

But anyway, the quick summary of what we're trying to get across is that there is no one "hardest part" about college for everyone; but, figure out how to budget your time effectively and everything else should be smooth sailing - except of course for midterms, finals, relationship problems, hangovers, STD's, and the occasional nervous breakdown you'll suffer when a computer virus attacks your hard drive and erases your 20-page paper the same night you find out your roommate hooked up with your ex-

-- The College Guy

QUESTION:

Ok. How can I get laid by the linebacker of our football team? It's not like i'm a 4 eyed freak with braces. A lot of guys have said i'm the hottest girl they've ever seen. I'm tall, blonde, blue eyes, skinny, love to watch football. So help me out here.

-- Lusting for Linebacker, UT

ANSWER:

First of all, let's not be so quick to pre-judge all the ugly, 4-eyed freaks out there – they have feelings too!

Second of all, forget about the linebacker on your football team! The real question is... How do you feel about quick-witted, overly-sarcastic, often-trying-too-hard-to-be-funny, advice columnists?

You can come to AskTheCollegeGuy.com Headquarters and be our tight end *or* our wide receiver - your choice!

-- The College Guy

QUESTION:
I graduated already but my girlfriend is still there (a senior). I feel like people view me as a loser if I'm still hanging out on campus and going to her date parties. So what do I do?

                                                              -- Bill, Delaware

ANSWER:
First of all, let us commend you on your perceptiveness. You are most likely correct - some people probably do view you as a loser for hanging around the undergrad scene now that you've graduated. Heck, for all we know you might actually be a loser. I mean, you've become "that guy." [*Note: The "That Guy" phenomenon can refer to many different situations - most of which are negative - but the specific one we're talking about here generally manifests itself at a bar, club, party, etc. when others point and whisper things to their friends like, "Hey, didn't that guy graduate already?"*]

Second of all, we're going to give you the benefit of the doubt that when you say you "graduated already" you mean that you just graduated in the last year or two and you're not some shady 30-something.

So, assuming the President that took office while you were in school was George W. Bush and not his father, we'll continue and assume that you're only a year or two older than your girlfriend.

Now, with all that said, if you still want to keep this girl as your girlfriend and hang around her when she's with her friends in what is now her world, you've got to be OK with the fact that people might be viewing you that way. It's probably a shot to your ego and it most likely makes you feel a little uncomfortable at times, but that's a sacrifice you've got to be OK with as a graduate with a girlfriend still in college.

Of course, there is an alternative - and the results with this alternate strategy will vary tremendously based on the level of trust you have in your relationship. You could always opt to completely separate yourself from her college world and let her go off with her friends and bring other guys to parties and date functions and just hope that she keeps coming back to you. But of course that all depends on a) how strong your relationship is, b) how much you trust her, and c) how much of a horny slut she turns into when you're not around.

Whether you continue to hang out with her on campus and at undergrad parties (as "that guy") basically depends on just how confident you are that she's not going to find someone better out on a dance floor somewhere.... But our real answer to this question would probably be that we don't have enough information about you, her, or your relationship to advise intelligently on your question. Write back with more info or just let us know how it all turns out.

-- *The College Guy*

QUESTION:
So I have this problem. The girl I've been dating is real hot, real fun, loves to bone, and doesn't really bug me to do shit for her all the time. You'd think I have it made, right? Well, the problem is that one of her roommates is even hotter and has this crazy sex appeal to her that is irresistible, especially to me. We flirt and party together and nothing has really ever come of it, but there have been those "moments" where something could have, and we both smiled and backed away slowly. Now, without ruining my relationship with my current girlfriend, without destroying their friendship, and without both of them dragging my name through the shit, how do I bang the friend, keep everything cool with the current, and let this chase finally be over?

-- *Wanting Them Both, Ohio State*

ANSWER #1:

So how does it feel to know that you single-handedly represent a huge part of the reason why guys get a bad wrap as being jerks, assholes, and chauvinistic pigs? Didn't anybody ever teach you the expression "you can't have your cake and eat it too," or do you consider yourself to be such an irresistible stud that you should be able to get whatever you want, whenever you want, from whoever you want?

Our advice: Take a cold shower, forget about girl #2, and try to appreciate what you've got in girl #1. There's always going to be a hotter girl out there somewhere, but if you're in any kind of committed relationship with your current girlfriend, it's your responsibility to ignore other temptations. By the way, do you think your girlfriend couldn't be nailing a better looking guy than you if she wanted to? Of course she could! Picture yourself finding out that she was gettin' the hot beef injection from your roommate or one of your other buddies. If that pisses you off, think about the fact you'd be doing the same thing to her. And if that idea doesn't bother you, then you've got some serious issues and you shouldn't be in this relationship in the first place.

ANSWER #2:

So you want to pull the "Hottie Roomie Double Juggle" and walk away unscathed with your reputation and current relationship both solidly intact? Wow! Talk about lofty goals! While the payoff would undoubtedly be huge (in addition to the sexual satisfaction, you'll also have stories to entertain your buddies with for years), the risks are even bigger. It's like sitting down at a black jack table and putting your entire life savings on the line for one hand. You could hit the jackpot and walk away a hero, or you could lose it all and wish you hadn't been such an arrogant, bone-headed jackass. [Editors' Note: Chances of success in said hand of black jack are slightly less than 50%. But even the smoothest, Van Wilder-like player on campus has less than a 10% chance of successfully pulling off the Hottie-Roomie-Double-Juggle without the situation blowing up in his face.]

Your question asks how to accomplish this feat "without ruining my relationship with my current girlfriend, without destroying their friendship, and without both of them dragging my name through the shit." Unfortunately, this is a very dangerous and delicate situation so if you decide to go for it, you're going to have to be prepared for all of those things to happen. Sorry. No risk means no reward. [*Editors' Note: Since AskTheCollegeGuy.com does not condone cheating of any kind, with the possible exception of revenge cheating if you were cheated on first, we can't actually give you advice for how to make this work -- although a good start would definitely be to make sure the roommate realizes she has as much to lose as you do if anybody were to find out about the whole thing. Anyway, like we were saying, we can't give you advice on how to make this work, but please, please, please write us back and let us know how it all turns out (and let us know what school you're transferring to after it blows up in your face)*]

-- ***The College Guy***

QUESTION:
i've been promiscuous in the past, being kept all sheltered up, until I broke free and ran away from mom and dads home at age 18.... I had my fun, by having sex, 3-somes, and what-not, but now im kinda interested in this guy, but he knows my past as well.... I wanna ask him out, but ive fucked him before, and ive fucked his friends before and he gets what he wants from me...but I want more. hes not in a relationship, and I dont really know much about him b/c we're just sex-buddies...HELP! .

-- ***Dunno What To Do, Brooklyn Community College***

ANSWER:

Lions, tigers, and bears don't make good pets.

Sluts, whores, and promiscuous skanks don't make good girlfriends.

If you'll nail anything with a pulse and a penis, why would he want you as his girlfriend? He can just call you, get his rocks off, and not worry about dating or, gulp, cuddling!

Start fresh, find a new guy, and play a little harder to get. And buy a frickin' vibrator if you need to!

-- The College Guy

Chapter Twelve
-AUGUST-

QUESTION:

I am going to be entering my freshman year and I was wondering how I am going to deal with living with a roommate and being able to still masturbate? Should I approach my new roommate and agree on a policy of in-room masturbating or should I just avoid the topic and hope I can keep quiet at night?

-- Incoming Freshman, Vanderbilt

ANSWER:

[Editors' Note: AskTheCollegeGuy.com recently commissioned a scientific study which showed that 96% of all college-aged males admit to masturbating; the study concluded that the remaining 4% are liars.]

Whether you are Zashir the Tanzanian goat herder or that guy from Nantucket that we've all heard so much about, masturbation is the silent bond that ties all post-pubescent males together. However, we haven't dubbed it the SILENT bond for nothing. While it is true that all men spank the monkey, toot their own horn, or stroke the hairless weasel, it is still often considered a taboo topic for open dialogue -- especially with someone you've just met.

Even if your new roommate is the kind of guy who is comfortable discussing the waving of the wonder wand, just imagine this scenario... You've just finished watching old Family Guy episodes and now you're ready to retire to your bed and allow yourself to imagine that a horny Meg Griffin is right there waiting for you. You strip down, climb up to your top bunk and are ready to lead your purple-helmeted warrior into battle. But wait, your roommate is right below you trying to catch some Z's before his big Bio test in the morning. No problem, you just lean over and say, "Hey Tom, I'm about to begin diagnostic testing on my heat-seeking moisture missile, so if the bed starts to shake or your hear any moaning, groaning, or crying, don't worry it's just me working the stick-shift, slapping the salami, petting the one-eyed monster... so you can just go back to sleep."

Well, gee, Tom is sure to ace that Bio test now! And you'd better believe every one of his stories the next day is going to start with, "Last night, my frickin' roommate.... "

So to all of you would-be public-whackers, when the time comes to sharpen the spear, you might want to do it behind a locked door - when you know your roommate isn't around. Additionally, the shower, a toilet stall, or even the library on a Friday night might provide more of a private setting with less risk of disturbing/offending your roommate. But for those of you who can only get in the mood while snugly tucked in bed, you'd better learn to be as quiet as a new fish in prison... 'cuz while guys all know *what* goes on, nobody wants to know *while* it's going on.

-- *The College Guy*

QUESTION:
I've heard college called the best 4 years of your life, but I don't really see it. Am I missing something?

                                    -- Shannon, Hofstra

ANSWER:
Yes, you are *definitely* missing something!

You know the expression, "You never know what you've got til it's gone"? We guarantee it was coined by a 23-year-old, suffering a quarter-life crisis, a year after graduating from college.

So anyway, what's so great about college life that you won't be able to fully appreciate until after graduation? Where to begin, where to begin....

[Note: You may have seen lists similar to this one on various websites and floating around via email forwards (so we apologize to anyone who wants to claim they are the true author of any of the following), but we've received a version of the email no less than 47 times from different people and not once have we seen an author's name attached. So we decided to put our own twist on it and pass it on to you]

Once you're done with college:

* 6:00 a.m. is when you get up, not when you go to sleep
* 20 hours a week is no longer a "full-load"
* You go from 130 days of vacation time to 7
* Sandals and flip-flops won't cut it anymore
* Your friends will marry and divorce instead of hook-up and break-up
* The idea of sex in a twin-sized bed will seem absurd
* You'll have more bills and you'll file your own taxes

* You'll actually be embarrassed if the only thing in your fridge is beer and 2-day-old pizza
* You'll be even more embarrassed if the only beer you have is Milwaukee's Best or Natural Light.
* Jeans and a button-down no longer qualify as "dressed up"
* You won't know what time Taco Bell closes anymore (and what's worse, you won't care)
* When you want to order pizza, you'll actually have to look up the number
* You don't necessarily live within walking distance of all your best friends
* Chicken wings, pizza, or even frozen yogurt at 3:00 a.m. will severely upset your stomach
* You go to the drugstore for Tylenol/Advil or Pepto/Tums, not condoms and Doritos
* A $4.00 bottle of wine is no longer "pretty good stuff"
* You actually eat breakfast foods at breakfast time
* "I just can't drink the way I used to", replaces "I'm never going to drink that much again"
* Finding a job sucks.
* Working sucks.
* Let us repeat that, Working (a real job) SUCKS!
* Showing up late and hung-over for work isn't the same as showing up late and hung-over for class.
* Skipping work isn't as easy as skipping class.
* You no longer take naps from noon to 6:00 PM...
* Actually, naps don't really exist at all after college.

The best advice you'll ever get from The College Guy:
Enjoy every moment of college while it lasts..... Every keg party, every hangover, every booty-call, every late-night cram session before finals, every minute of dorm life, every intramural sporting event... Enjoy it All!

-- *The College Guy*

QUESTION:

How do you tell your boyfriend - subtly - that even though you may love him to bits, that he's shit in bed and that you'd actually prefer listening to the not-so-attractive-asshole-down-the-hall spanking the monkey than the thought of having to get back into bed with him?

                    -- Not-so-subtle, Southampton UK

ANSWER:

So your super-stud is a super-dud? And he's sooooo bad that you'd prefer the soothing sounds of Jacko The Chronic Masturbator than spend some between-the-sheets time with your dude? OUCH!!!

Well, there is no easy way to say this, so we'll incorporate some audience participation. Here's what we want you to do. Get up and walk to the bathroom. Then look in the mirror. Then repeat these words: "Mirror, mirror, on the wall, who's at fault for my unsatisfying sex life?" [Editors' Note: We all know this is the question Disney really had in mind for Snow White... C'mon, you don't really buy that "who's the fairest one of all" crap, do you?]

Anyway, we here at AskTheCollegeGuy.com guarantee that your magic mirror will show you the person who is responsible for your dilemma.

What the F@%#!!! The only thing you see in the mirror is you??!!!??

YAHTZEE! We're sorry to deflate your ego, but if your man isn't driving you to O-town (or even a suburb anywhere near that elusive destination), look no further than yourself for the reason why. Now, before you flip out and go on the defensive, please let us explain. While all men like to think they could bring a potted plant to orgasm if given the right Barry White album, truth be told there are plenty of guys out there who couldn't find there way around down there with a *Maxim* and a flashlight. That is why the burden falls on the ladies to help out with a little direction.

Each woman has her own likes and dislikes, certain things that drive each one to ... well... at least to a point where you'd rather be back in bed with your guy than listening to Jacko The Chronic Masturbator down the hall. What your not-so-dexterous dude did with his last girlfriend may have driven her wild, while it leaves you as cold as a fish at market. [Editors' Note: Let's stay away from "fish" analogies when talking about certain subject matter in future columns.]

So you need to use your mouth (for something other than half-hearted moans intended to fake pleasure and end your misery) and you need to communicate. Next time, don't be afraid to give a little coaching where needed. Tell him when he does something that feels good and ask that he keep doing it. And when he repeats something else that produces as much pleasure as repetitive tapping on your forehead, let him know that too. And don't be afraid to set the tempo and suggest different positions you might enjoy. Either your man will be responsive to your tutoring and any new ideas you bring to the bedroom, which will make all the difference in the world, or he'll refuse to acknowledge that me might not be as innately talented as he thinks and you'll eventually dump the stubborn mule and one of you will end up hanging out with Jacko the Chronic Masturbator down the hall.

-- The College Guy

QUESTION:

Okay.. here's the deal.. I'm a virgin waiting for love and all the guys I've been in relationships with for the past two years seem only to be in the relationships for sex. Now.. I guess what I'm asking is... are there actually good/decent guys out there who actually care about the relationship and not the actual sex? cause if not, i'm guessing i'm screwed...

   -- Virgin looking for nice guy, College of Charleston

ANSWER:

This is a funny coincidence because one of our AskTheCollegeGuy.com staff members has been having wet dreams about a girl like you for the past four years! (He's looking for a virgin so she won't have any other guys to compare him to - that way she'd never know he's hung like a hamster). Send us a photo of yourself and we'll try to set you two up!

Okay, we're going to be serious for a minute here.... We get a dozen letters a week from guys complaining they can't meet a nice girl and another two dozen from girls complaining they can't meet a nice guy. The real problem isn't that there aren't quality people out there, it's just that it's REALLY TOUGH TO MEET THEM. Look around next time you're in class (or at least the next time you're in class and you're not hung over, barely able to keep your eyes open) - how many of your classmates might have potential? A lot of them! You just have to find new and creative ways to meet them. Good guys are out there - good girls are out there - just take advantage of every opportunity you get to talk to them (*before and after class, in line at the post office…your opportunities are almost endless*)

And one more thing, specifically regarding your question of looking for a "good/decent guy who actually cares about the relationship and not just the sex" ... While those good/decent guys do exist, they're not necessarily going to be the loudest, most visible guys on campus and they might tend to be a little shy -- so that's why you might have to look a little harder to find one, because they won't necessarily be the ones throwing out cheesy pick-up lines at bars or hitting on every girl that crosses their path.

-- The College Guy

QUESTION:
Dear college guy,
I am having issues. I broke up with my boyfriend over a year ago, and since then I haven't had any sex... I don't know what to do... I'm going crazy... I was a virgin before my last boyfriend, but now its like the sexual frustration is 10 times worse than it was when I was a virgin. I want sex, but I don't want a 1 night stand, and I really don't want a full blown relationship.

-- Sexually Frustrated in Northern California

ANSWER:
Suggestion #1: The first thing you need to do is send us a picture of yourself. If we like what we see, we'll send you directions to AskTheCollegeGuy.com headquarters (picture the Bat Cave, only not as cool) and when you get here, we'd be more than happy to help you take care of your little problem.

Now, if we don't like your picture (or more likely, you have no intention of actually sending us your picture), we've got some other suggestions for you...

Suggestion #2: We completely understand that you don't want to have a one-night stand. So we suggest you find a totally random guy at a bar, put your hand on his inner thigh, tell him you're extremely horny and that you want to have sex with him. But, you tell him that there is one condition: he needs to have sex with you both tonight AND tomorrow night. That way, by definition, it's not a one-night stand.

Suggestion #3: Ok, if you're afraid that our previous suggestion might end up hurting your reputation, then we've got one more, slightly different suggestion. Take the same approach as above, except don't go for a random guy in a bar. Go to the library and find a semi-dorky looking guy who doesn't necessarily look like the prototypical, alpha-male, chick-magnet. When he picks his head up from his Chemistry book, explain to him how horny you are and that you want to take him back to your place for a night of hot passion and pleasure. And don't worry about word getting out about a one-night stand with this guy because, if you pick a dorky enough guy, nobody will believe his story anyway so your reputation is safe.
                                                        -- The College Guy

P.S. We just had a really crazy idea pop into our head. It might be a long-shot, but it would be the perfect solution to your problem! This might be a little unrealistic, but here goes... Ok, so you want sex but you don't want a one-night stand and you don't want a full-blown relationship. Well, what if... just WHAT IF you could find a guy who was also interested in just having sex?

We realize such a guy would be one-in-a-million because most college guys are only looking for serious, committed, monogamous relationships where they get to go shopping with their girlfriends instead of hanging out with the guys. *[Editors' Note: If you did not recognize the previous sentence as complete and utter sarcasm, you are not allowed to continue reading this book. Please put the book down, go put on your running shoes, go outside, and then sprint directly into a brick wall.]* But anyway, do you think you might be able to find that rare guy who wants the sex, but not the relationship? A guy who would have sex with you as often as you want, but then would go play ball or drink beers with the guys instead of cuddling and spending the night like a real boyfriend?

Again, we know this could be very very difficult to find a guy who is just interested in sex. But we think that if you look around campus really hard, there's a chance you just might be able to find that one-in-a-million guy who's willing to forego all the dating stuff just to have sex with you. Good luck and let us know how the quest goes.

QUESTION:

I've been dating my girlfriend off and on for three years now. Before her, I had only had sex with one other girl. For some reason, I am becoming extremely bothered by her past promiscuity and it is hurting our relationship because I dont think I want to be with her anymore. How can I forget things she has done in the past because it is ruining a relationship that otherwise would be great?

-- Troubled by Promiscuity, University of Florida

ANSWER:

Ok, first of all, you've definitely gotta GET OVER IT!!!! We realize that's easier said than done, so you can either wait until March 9th for National "Get Over It Day" (www. GetOverItDay.com) or you can keep reading and hope that we can help. Either way, the first step is to really think about why it bothers you so much in the first place.

- ✓ Are you afraid you're not satisfying her in the sack as well as some of her past partners?
- ✓ Are you afraid that she just doesn't share the same morals as you?

- ✓ Are you afraid that the sex won't mean as much to her as it does to you?
- ✓ Are you afraid that she'll cheat on you now or in the future?
- ✓ Are you afraid people will think less of you for dating a dirty skank?
- ✓ Are you afraid you'll contract a scorching case of the itchy-scratchies?

You are definitely afraid of SOMETHING! So you've gotta figure out the what, why, and how. Figure out exactly WHAT it is that you're afraid of so you can figure out WHY her past promiscuity is bothering you so much so you can figure out HOW to get over it and move ahead with a relationship that you are otherwise pretty stoked about. And if it's something that you really just can't get over, well, that sucks... but if you really like her, we don't recommend ending it without talking to her about it first -- give her a chance to at least lie to you and tell you you're the best she's ever had.

But seriously, you've gotta figure this out sooner rather than later... and nobody (not even the all-knowing AskTheCollegeGuy.com Team) can tell you what is specifically bothering you about the situation. Ask yourself the 6 "are you afraid" questions above... figure out the what, why, and how... and then hopefully you'll be able to get through this without ruining the relationship with your slut girlfriend.

-- *The College Guy*

P.S. If she's constantly yelling out a different guy's name during sex, that might be a sign of bigger problems that you might not be able to get over. (Just be sure to let us know if she's ever yells out "Oh, College Guy!")

QUESTION:
I'm a guy and me and my best girl friend are perfect together. I think we both know it, but we're scared to take it to the next level because if it doesn't work we're afraid it'll ruin the friendship.

> *-- Just a friend (for now), San Diego State*

ANSWER:
We here at AskTheCollegeGuy.com normally don't make movie recommendations because we realize that everyone has dramatically different tastes. So...

- ✓ If we recommend Billy Madison, Happy Gilmore, and Tommy Boy, we alienate the supposedly more mature crowd that thinks those movies are dumb and immature.
- ✓ If we recommend The Natural, Rudy, or Hoosiers, then we alienate the non-sports-fans.
- ✓ If we recommend Crouching Tiger Hidden Dragon or Life is Beautiful, we alienate the illiterate or lysdexic who can't read the sub-titles.
- ✓ If we recommend Remember the Titans, School Ties, Philadelphia, or Snow White and The Seven Dwarfs then we alienate the racists, anti-Semites, homophobes, and dwarf-haters.

... and our readership isn't big enough that we can afford to alienate anybody under the age of 30.

So what does this have to do with the question that was asked? Not much... other than the fact that we're going to make an untraditional move and recommend a movie. But don't worry, it's not really even a *good* movie, just appropriate to the question at hand. Go rent Boys and Girls (starring Freddie Prinz Jr., Claire Forlani, and Jason Biggs).

Again, we're not saying this is one of our all-time favorites or anything like that (at best, it's a solid NetFlixer), but it is absolutely a movie you should watch. It should help you think about the pros and cons of your situation.

And if you watch it with this "best girl friend" of yours, we predict incredible sexual tension (hopefully followed by incredible sex). Let us know how it turns out!

-- *The College Guy*

QUESTION:
Can you write me an essay on why you feel watching the movie "Billy Madison" makes you smater please!!!!!!!!!!!!!! it will mean a lot to me it only has to be like 200 words.

-- *Alyssa, University*

[Editors' Note: We'll assume you meant "smarter" and not "smater." And if watching Billy Madison does make you smarter, you have either never seen it or you need to watch it a few more times because for your "College/University," you entered: "yes". Thanks so much, but we were actually looking for specifically which *college or university you attend. Nonetheless, your question will be answered.]*

ANSWER:
Normally we don't take requests to "write an essay" on anything... But, this was an unusual request that brought a huge smile to the face of each AskTheCollegeGuy.com staff member who read it. So you're not going to actually get an essay from us - because that would make us "your bitch", and we've repeatedly stated over the years that "we ain't nobody's bitch", but we will answer your question and give you your 200 words on why watching Billy Madison makes you smarter.

TOP 5 LESSONS LEARNED FROM BILLY MADISON:

1. You learn your colors (Miss Lippy's car is Green).
2. You learn about classic Literature (like the Great American Novel entitled: The Puppy Who Lost His Way)
3. You learn that bullies are bad (O'Doyle does NOT rule).
4. You learn compassion for others (doesn't it bring a tear to your eye watching Billy splash water on his own crotch to protect little Ernie from public ridicule?).
5. You learn that if you work really hard in third grade, you've got a shot at hooking up with your super-hot teacher. Note: In real life, Veronica Vaughn is played by Bridgette Wilson and she's married to tennis star Pete Sampras. DAMN HIM! He's one of the best tennis players in the world, he's a multi-millionaire, and he gets to touch Veronica Vaughn's heiney??? Rot in hell Pete Sampras - It's just not fair!!!

-- The College Guy

QUESTION:

If I get into a relationship with a man who is about to go on tour for a month, do you think he can remain faithful.

-- Phat Sugar, USC

ANSWER:

Dear Phat Sugar,

Are you an English major? If so then you'll understand the importance of choosing the correct verb when you ask a question. *Can* he remain faithful? Of course he *can*. But *will* he remain faithful? That's an entirely different question which depends on too many factors for even the all-knowing College Guy to answer definitively. *[Note: Among the factors it depends on would be - how cool are you? how hot are you? and how good are you in the sack?]*

And what the hell does "on tour" mean anyway? Is he a soldier going on a military tour of duty? Is he a musician going on tour with a band? If it's the former you've got a decent chance that he'll remain faithful. If it's the latter, our Magic 8-ball says "Fat Chance, Phat Sugar."

-- The College Guy

QUESTION:
My guy respects me and all (at least I think...) but he never acts like he loves me and he never calls me or visits me or... kisses me or hugs me. What should I do???
-- Not Getting Enough Affection, Univ. of Tennessee

ANSWER:
We, here at AskTheCollegeGuy.com, have given a lot of thought to your dilemma. You might not like our advice, but here it is anyway. The first thing you must do is: Make sure your boyfriend is real and not just a figment of your imagination. This "boyfriend reality check" can be done in a number of ways:

- ✓ Ask your friends if they have ever seen or talked to your boyfriend.
- ✓ Take a look around your room and see if you have any photos of your boyfriend that are not cut out of magazines.
- ✓ When out in public with your boyfriend, try and notice if people start looking at you funny or if you hear anyone ask, "Who are you talking too?" when you and your boyfriend are conversing.

If by some chance you come to find out that your boyfriend is actually real, then you can move on to step number two which is to dump his sorry ass. We know that every girl dreams of one day finding a guy who never calls, never writes, never stops by and doesn't want to have any kind of physical or emotional connection; but all we are saying is that maybe this particular thoughtless no-show just isn't the right thoughtless no-show for you.

And if this clown-of-a-boyfriend you've described actually is real, we find it more than likely that you'll get more enjoyment out of a pretend boyfriend (particularly the battery-operated ones) than the super-dud you are describing. We can only assume this guy must have some redeeming qualities or you wouldn't be with him in the first place, so if you're not ready to completely give up on Mr. NeverThere, give him one last chance. Tell him that it bothers you that "he never acts like he loves me and he never calls me or visits me or... kisses me or hugs me." Tell him you need more than what he's giving. Let him know how much it bothers you. If you lay it all on the line, either he'll change and start giving you more attention, or he won't change and then it'll be easier for you to cut your losses and dump his sorry ass for a guy with a few more tangible qualities. You deserve better, so either force him to be better, or move on and find better.

-- The College Guy

QUESTION:
Why is my girlfriend so damn weird? Seriously, sometimes I think she's legally insane.

-- Kurt, Kansas State

ANSWER:
Surprisingly, Kurt, we don't actually know your girlfriend (unless she was that cute little red-head in the black mini-skirt, white tube-top, and leopard-print thong that was

dancing on the bar at AskTheCollegeGuy.com headquarters last night).

Since you've given virtually no details or examples for why you think your girlfriend is a few beers short of a 6-pack, even the all-knowing AskTheCollegeGuy.com writers and editors can't venture a guess. So, in addition to using your vague question to remind all our readers to PROVIDE DETAILS in all future questions, we're going to use your question to vent/hypothesize about why people are so screwed up these days in general - regardless of whether or not this actually applies to your girlfriend.

WHY PEOPLE ARE SO SCREWED UP:
Imagine that you are a parent and for some reason you come up with this sick, twisted, demented plot to really screw up your kids and make them nuts. What would you do? How would you go about raising a kid to intentionally try to increase the likelihood that they grow up to be really screwed up?

Here are a few ways that a parent could really screw with a kid's head - if the parent really had evil intentions:

- ✓ Force your kids to watch "educational" television shows that feature a big talking-bird and a little green grouchy guy who lives in a trash can. Because if that doesn't educate them about the real world, we don't know what will.
- ✓ Let your kids watch cartoons of little blue people who live in a village of mushroom houses - and then, if little blue people living in mushrooms aren't weird enough, try to convince your kid that the one and only girl who lives in that village isn't a whore. We're not saying Smurfette wasn't hot

(actually, we'd smurf the sh*t out of her if given half a chance), but she just wasn't necessarily the poster-child for monogamy.

✓ Tell your kids that once a year, a big fat guy in a red suit will fly around on magic reindeer and slide down chimneys to bring gifts to all the little children - except, of course, the children of those silly Jews, Muslims, and anybody else who doesn't happen to share certain religious beliefs.

✓ Tell your kids that when they lose a tooth they should put it under their pillow and a magical fairy will come, take the tooth, and give them money in return. *[Editors' Note: We firmly believe that it is this whole "Tooth Fairy" practice that subconsciously increases the likelihood of children growing up to become porn stars or prostitutes. Think about it... by giving money to a kid for their teeth, you're basically encouraging them to use their body for money!]*

Anyway, those are some things that could really f*ck with a kid's sanity during the crucial developmental years of childhood. And people still wonder why there are so many weirdos out there.

-- *The College Guy*

ABOUT THE AUTHOR

Believe it or not, this has been the hardest page of the book to write. Part of the success of AskTheCollegeGuy.com over the years has been due to the somewhat mysterious cloak of anonymity afforded by the internet. Nobody really ever knew the identity of the sarcastically condescending wiseass known only as "The College Guy."

But, contrary to what our name may indicate, there is not one single "guy" who dispenses all of AskTheCollegeGuy. com's words of wisdom/sarcasm/advice/entertainment. Rather, the voice of "the college guy" is actually a carefully crafted compilation of advice and humor from a team of contributing writers, comprised of students (both male and female) and recent graduates (both male and female) from colleges and universities around the country.

Content is all woven together (anonymously until now) by a team of editors, led by Jeff Goldblatt, the owner and Managing Editor of AskTheCollegeGuy.com. *[Note: You might not know his name, but you've probably heard his voice. Jeff is best known as creator and voice of the world-famous Rejection Hotline, www.RejectionHotline.com]* Anyway, the finished product is distributed under the mysteriously anonymous, all-knowing, sarcastic voice of "The College Guy".

www.AskTheCollegeGuy.com

SPECIAL THANKS

Special thanks to all of the following for their contributions, suggestions, ideas, and support:

- Cara Pitterman

- J.P. Bartonico

- Jason Costa

- Timothy Lemke

- Juliana Mims

- Emily Bull *

- Jeff Goldblatt *

- Scott Slotnick

- Jennifer Berry

- Hanna Fetveit

- Robbie Foote

- Joel Harrison

- Kristy Sterling

- All our friends and family

- And to anyone else we did not mention by name, THANK YOU! *(email us and we'll issue a public correction/apology for forgetting to mention you)*

*All materials edited by Emily Bull and Jeff Goldblatt.

www.ingramcontent.com/pod-product-compliance
Lightning Source LLC
Chambersburg PA
CBHW030321290526
45785CB00001B/463